Kingdom Finances

How to Access God's Wealth in Your Daily Living

Hector Ramos

ISBN 978-1-63885-918-5 (Paperback)
ISBN 978-1-63885-919-2 (Digital)

Note: The New King James Version of the Bible is used in this book.

Covenant Books
11661 Hwy 707
Murrells Inlet, SC 29576
www.covenantbooks.com

To my wife, Suzanna Jeyanthi Ramos, without whom this book would have taken years longer to write. She is key to the development and production of this work because the fruit of our lives together gave me the inspiration to write the following pages.

Contents

Foreword

Sowing and reaping. Giving and receiving. Stewardship. Offerings. Tithes. These are just some of the words that come to my mind when I think about finances. I had the distinct privilege of growing up around a particular movement that afforded me the opportunity to learn from an early age key principles regarding finances. It was in this same movement that I also grew to dislike offering time in churches, messages on finances, and anything to do with church and money. Anytime someone would get up to take an offering, I would find myself in utter disgust for what would happen. That is until I met Dr. Hector Ramos.

The first time I heard Dr. Ramos teach on Kingdom Finances, I was unsure whether to grab my notebook or my checkbook. There was so much revelation in what he shared and not one bit of manipulation. Over time, I have been so humbled to work with Hector on a ministry level, eventually inviting him and his wife to be the associate pastors at our church.

I have also learned that Hector doesn't take anything lightly. He sees the importance of words and what he says and how it is applied to our lives. Perhaps this is why it took years to get this book into your hands. When I read the initial manuscript, I wept. I was finally holding something in my hands that I knew could change the landscape of giving in the American and even Western churches.

My prayer is that just as I was convicted as I read, you would be too. This book holds principles and keys that will transform your life. I know this because I have observed Dr. Ramos teach them for years, and they have transformed mine. Read. Engage. Give. Be transformed.

Jacob Biswell, ThM
Senior pastor
The Equipping Church

Acknowledgments

I would like to thank the following for helping, supporting, and mentoring and for inviting me and my wife, Suzanna, to partner with them in ministry.

Jacob Biswell (senior pastor, The Equipping Church, Bryan, Texas) has been a beacon and encouraged me to produce this volume. He even mentioned it in one of his sermons. His patience and endurance are of the Holy Spirit. As a prophet to the nations, Pastor Jacob's endorsement and validation of the theology presented here are very much appreciated.

Cristobal Ledezma (senior pastor, Casa de Dios Ministries, Bryan, Texas) saw in me a gift for speaking to the church about tithes and offerings. For many years, he has helped me develop the revelations written here. He opened the way for me to minister, preach, teach, and become a catalyst for Casa de Dios Ministries, a blessing to nations.

Rev. Dr. Amos Jayarathnam (senior overseer, Tabernacle of Holiness, Singapore), a true father in the faith, helped us during many years of our work in the United States. He welcomed me and Suzanna into his ministry in Indonesia, Estonia, Russia, Malaysia, India, and the United States. That involvement helped us grow in the gifts of the Spirit and find God's purpose for us.

Rev. Xavier Dawes (senior pastor, Tabernacle of Holiness, Singapore), a humble servant of God, encouraged us and gave us the wisdom to overcome great relational obstacles in ministry.

Introduction

You might be asking yourself, "Why one more Christian book?"

My easy answer is, "It has been written because the Lord told me so."

However, the motivation behind this book goes further. Mine has been a journey of disobedience, conviction, more conviction brought on by prophets and prophetic people, more disobedience, and then repentance and reaching out for the grace necessary to write this book. I believe with all my heart that you will see the grace of God in this book, which made the impossible possible.

You may also be asking yourself, "Why one more book on finances?" More books have been written to justify greed *by faith* than to deal with God's provision for His family and kingdom. There is a river of deceptive *Christian* books that promise to reveal the formula for prosperity, depicting God as a clerk in heaven's treasury rather than a Father who loves His creation. We need more books to help us increase in discernment and to distinguish idolatry of mammon (i.e., the love of money) from the righteous use of the wealth with which God has blessed us.

This book is not only about words of revelation but also a process of understanding. We need to grow accustomed to finding tools that will help us inquire about and receive much more than before. The challenge is not only from the perspective of understanding ("I know what the Bible says") but also from wisdom ("I know what to do with it"). This should compel us to action like never before. The principle of scripture explaining scripture guides the explanation that follows. This is just the beginning of your adventure. I pray that reading the following words will challenge you to dig deeper and seek treasures in the Bible because they are there waiting for you to find them, through prayer and study.

I was called by my pastor many years ago to share revelations regarding tithes and offerings. I have been doing the same work for the last nine years in the different churches to which the Lord has brought me. This time of sharing has been refreshing for many who continue to trust in the Lord, and a concealed clarion call to join the laborers bringing in the harvest.

I want to thank you for sowing seeds by buying this book. I appreciate the trust you have given me, and I pray that the Lord will show much more to you and that the following pages will be a trigger for revelation and obedience, making it possible for you to see His provision at work in your life so that you will fulfill the purpose He has for you.

I would like to express my gratitude to my wife Suzanna Ramos, who has continually and kindly reminded me of the urgent need to write this book. I also give thanks to my pastor, Jacob Biswell, in joining my wife in prophetically and lovingly pushing me forward to have this work published. I hope they both partake in the harvest this book will bring, to the glory of God. It takes God's patience and endurance to convince people to invest in what God has called them to do. I have had the privilege of helping many build such virtues. Finally, I want to thank all the prophets and prophetic people who have encouraged me and shared their time and finances such that this project has been realized.

At the end of this book, I have included a list of resources that will help you and your church move forward in the realm of kingdom building.

Pastor Dr. Hector Ramos

Section I

The Heart and Mind of the Sower

In this section, you will receive revelations regarding different aspects of giving. As you know, the Lord speaks to us about giving Him praise and thanksgiving, apart from tithes and offerings. In fact, the Bible encourages us to go beyond this in our giving by giving our lives to the kingdom of God. This revelation is foundational, and this foundational truth of complete sacrifice unto God will give you the right perspective on the facets discussed below. Otherwise, you may make the same mistake as many have in the past. You may look for a quick fix, a formula, or anything else that will help you get God to bless you by your works and not your faith.

If you want to receive from God as a son or daughter, you will need to relate to Him as your Father. This means a desire for separation from the world, to worship and show obedience unto Him. The key to developing such an attitude is to know that everything comes from Him. He will help you to do His will and act to please Him (Philippians 2.13). Your effort to trust and show obedience will become effortless, for you know that God is exceptionally good. In fact, He is so good that He delights in blessing you as His son or daughter. You don't have to convince Him or manipulate Him into doing that.

My prayer is that as you read this book prayerfully and put into action what the Lord reveals to you through it. He will show up in your life like never before and lead you to true prosperity. Every chapter is designed to bring something fresh to you and your desire to know Him ever more intimately. If your desire is for financial wealth more than for God, may this book be a source of repentance and change so you can be free to receive the abundance of things He has for you. If you want your bank account to be full, decide today to make your account His account. From that moment, your giving will become joyful.

We need to change our minds about His kingdom and finances, but we also need to convert our hearts. May this book bring both changes into your life that you will feel His heart and hear His good thoughts and know the plan He has for you.

Chapter 1

Kingdom of God

But seek first the kingdom of God and His righteousness, and all these things shall be added to you. Matthew 6:33

But if I cast out devils by the Spirit of God, then the kingdom of God is come unto you. Matthew 12:28

But without faith it is impossible to please Him, for he who comes to God must believe that He is, and that He is a rewarder of those who diligently *seek Him*. Hebrews 11:6

Jesus answered him, "The *first of all* the commandments is: 'Hear, O Israel, the Lord our God, the Lord is one. And you shall love the Lord your God with all your heart, with all your soul, with all your mind, and with all your strength.' This is the first commandment. And the second, like it, is this: 'You shall love your neighbor as yourself.' There is no other commandment greater than these." Mark 12:29–31

It isn't what we don't know that gives us trouble,
it's what we know that ain't so.

—Will Rogers

The foundations of the scripture show us that God is love, and He wants to reveal His love through us. This is done through a process of not only seeking and loving Him but also by loving others. Seeking Him *not only* leads us to prayer, fasting, praise, and the study of His Word. It also leads us to obedience to Him through service to others. If we speak and act toward others in faith, we bring a blessing to each other that the Holy Spirit can use to impact the people around us.

Another foundational aspect of His kingdom is power. He was not being selective when he said that His people will demonstrate His power as they go in His name to speak His message. When the Lord's Word, presence, and power touch you, it is for you to receive so that you can bring that blessing to others. The Samaritan woman brought a message to a village that was full of power, healing, and deliverance; relationships were healed, and they were delivered from their own prejudices to receive Christ (John 4).

Seeking, loving, and experiencing Him to make Him known and experienced by others are the manifestations of His power through the message that He brings. This should be our utmost priority. This is faith in action.

Have you ever wondered about the main points Jesus was trying to convey regarding entering His kingdom? And how these points might relate to finances? There seems to be a significant blind spot that keeps us at a great distance from the profound destiny Jesus has ordained for everyone who calls upon His name. In Matthew 21:31, Jesus was talking to religious people who were fully persuaded that God had nothing against them and that they could keep their inheritance from the kingdom for themselves. However, Jesus points out that those who were despised by these people (e.g., tax collectors and prostitutes) had received salvation and were entering the kingdom of God *first*. Could this be a lesson for us? Could this be a part of the church today?

If we are to seek the Word and the Lord for revelation, we need to first have a healthy mindset for change. There may be things we take for granted that hinder us from moving forward. We want to love God but not others, we want His kingdom but not His power, and we want His blessings but not His will or dominion over us to bring a message of His love to others through sacrifice. Maybe our worship of God is compromised because we only believe in the church of one—me.

I suggest to you that there is a great need for revelation and obedience in this hour, not only to *know* what the Lord is speaking about but also to *experience* what He has promised. Jesus does not seem to be concerned with financing His work. In fact, He speaks and then the miracle happens. He wants His servants to do His work and produce spiritual fruit first. That fruit is an expression of His power and will. In fact, the Christian life is full of work with God, where God can be revealed:

> In the same way, let your light shine before others, that they may see your good deeds and glorify your Father in heaven. (Matthew 5:16)

The kingdom of God and the works of the kingdom are intimately related; they need to become our spiritual guide for us to experience God's provision in which "all these things shall be added to you" (Matthew 6:33). Don't make going to church a ritual activity or boring duty. Be intentional in your desire to meet with God and have fellowship with other believers. Learn from ministers so that you can be trained to do the work that God has for you. The Lord appreciates the small works that we do in His name. Your provision will be sent to you in ways that will amaze you.

If you really want God to take care of your financial problems in a supernatural way, you need to change your *mindset* and become focused on and concerned about the issues that matter to Him *first*: His kingdom come, His will be done, His glory to be made manifest on earth as it is in heaven (Matthew 6:10). If your investments of time, prayer, finances, and gifts are for His kingdom, you will see God's hand at work in those financial issues that concern you, threatening to make you a lifetime slave to debt. The Lord will not only provide for you, but He will also remove any affection and selfish ambition that you may have for possessions so that your heart will have only pure motivation for Him. When He has removed your hidden love of money, you will see that being wealthy will not endanger your worship. You will become a distributor of God's wealth.

Prayer:
Father, make me see myself as a worker in Your vineyard. Let me appreciate and honor those You have sent to train me to do the work and let me recognize the spiritual fruit that will remain and glorify Your name.

Further Reading

> And again I say unto you, It is easier for a camel to go through the eye of a needle, than for a rich man to enter into the kingdom of God. Matthew 19:24

> Whether of them twain did the will of his father? They say unto him, "The first." Jesus saith unto them, "Verily I say unto you, That the publicans and the harlots go into the kingdom of God before you." Matthew 21:31

> Therefore say I unto you, The kingdom of God shall be taken from you, and given to a nation bringing forth the fruits thereof. Matthew 21:43

Chapter 2

Will of God

Beloved, I pray that you may prosper in all things and be in health, just as your soul prospers. 3 John 2:2

And you shall remember the LORD your God, for it is He who gives you power to get wealth, that He may establish His covenant which He swore to your fathers, as it is this day. Deuteronomy 8:18

Oh, give thanks to the Lord, for He is good! For His mercy endures forever. Psalm 136:1

Trust in the Lord with all your heart, and lean not on your own understanding; In all your ways acknowledge Him, and He shall direct your paths. Proverbs 3:5–6

The Bible says that the Lord is *good*, and His mercy endures forever. It is because of His goodness that He delights in providing for His children. To completely surrender to Him, we need to recognize that our understanding will not suffice; in fact, trusting in Him completely entails leaving behind our own understanding and perceiving

His direction for our path. It is a recognition that He is in charge, and we commit to Him our ways.

The Lord desires for you to prosper in *all* your ways. However, we tend to be shortsighted when looking for the blessings of the Lord. He has much more for us when we surrender all to Him. There are plans and ways of God that go beyond our small vision. Because He is such a good and powerful God, He wants His children also to have great vision. The work that the Lord can do through you can go beyond you. As you do His will, He will multiply the work that you do and enlarge your worth, impacting not only your family but also your region, nation, and many nations beyond. That was the promise given to Abraham, which the Lord wants to fulfill.

The Lord's will is found in His Word. He will show you more and more that He wants to fulfill the promises He has made to you. The primary challenge that the average Christian finds in doing the will of God is that you cannot do it without faith, and you cannot have faith without seeking God. Finally, you cannot seek God without prayer and the study of His Word. The constant prayer of the believer is daily bread. It is in that bread (i.e., the revelation of His Word) that you will feel the prompting of the Holy Spirit, for it is the Holy Spirit who works in you to do His will according to His good pleasure (Philippians 2:13).

It is the will of God that you prosper and have the power to create wealth (Deuteronomy 8:18). Your business success is important for God, fulfilling the covenant that He made with Abraham "that He may establish His covenant which He swore to your fathers" (Deuteronomy 8:18). He wants your success to speak to the promises given to Abraham. He wants your life to be a reflection and witness of His goodness. In this perspective, our wealth belongs to God, and it is for Him to use for His glory. If you can recognize that your success is God-given, then you can agree that your wealth belongs to Him. It will be easier for you to become God's distributor of wealth, meeting the needs of people through the power of God.

It has been my experience that the Lord is not just interested in us doing His will with His wealth. He wants to refine our hearts so that we have pure motivations to know that we need to ask ourselves and what are we after? What are our sources of satisfaction? What makes us happy? How do we feel fulfilled? Are those sources of motivation found in the world, in others, or in the Lord and doing His will? Can we say like Jesus did that we have come and been born again to do God's will? (Hebrews 10). In that chapter of Hebrews, we see how it was God's will to sacrifice His Son on the cross for our salvation. In the same way, we need to persevere in our belief in the salvation of the soul. Let the redeemed of the Lord say so; let them rejoice in their salvation. The preaching of the cross is the foundation of our testimony about salvation. That is the will of God for our lives. As we commit our ways to Him, He uses us to speak of the power of death and resurrection of Christ through our lives. Whatever we do speaks aloud of who Jesus is as it is the Holy Spirit who leads us to speak, bless our enemies, and overcome evil with good. It is He who leads us in seeking the Lord's hand through our words and actions, believing that He will confirm our work with the manifestation of His power.

Prayer:
Lord, I submit my ways to You today. I pray that You guide me and help me be obedient to You even though I may disagree with Your plan. Help me become obedient through love and trust in You. I pray that You establish my path and that people will see Your blessing in Your protection, provision, and the fulfillment of Your promises in my life.

Further Reading

The blessing of the Lord makes one rich, and He adds no sorrow with it. Proverbs 10:22

In everything give thanks; for this is the will of God in Christ Jesus for you. 1 Thessalonians 5:18

Chapter 3

Trust in God

He who trusts in his riches will fall, but the righteous will flourish like foliage. Proverbs 11:28

Trust in the Lord with all your heart, and lean not on your own understanding; In all your ways acknowledge Him, and He shall direct your paths. Proverbs 3:5–6

The place of your promise will first be the place of your affliction that you may be trained for your purpose in God. The Lord showed Abraham the place to go, yet he encountered famine. Joseph had to go through a challenging training journey to Egypt and be sold as a slave; he ended up serving and becoming a witness in prison. Isaac, Jacob, Daniel, David, Peter, Paul, and countless other servants of God have all gone through a similar process of trials and tribulations to learn to trust and obey the Lord, finding that place of fulfillment that God's call promised to them.

The same can be said about a business, church, or calling. Some prophets have called it the prophets in the training stage, or PITS. If you believe that you are called to be a fountain of finance for the church of Jesus Christ, He will call you to His purpose for the church as a whole. He *will* test your obedience to His voice in this area. You *will* need to trust Him for supernatural provision when there is no other way. His becoming your source will be a process that will brand your heart with fire. Your proclamation of His goodness will come from experiences that will break you and crush your desire for the things of the world. People will call you crazy to trust your God completely, but in your craziness, the Lord will be glorified, and they will declare that the Lord is truly with you. In that place of affliction, the Lord removes all our tendencies to find solutions in the world, such as through get-rich-quick money schemes. How many believers have put their faith in network marketing or multilevel businesses more than in God's provision? And because of His goodness, He will go before us even though some fall into these worldly temptations. He will deliver us and teach us a better way.

To learn to trust in the Lord completely means to stop trusting in backup plans altogether. This is because "plan B" is always based on doubt. Doubt and faith cannot live in the same household. Trust in God is deeply connected with faith and created by Him, His Word, and our response to it. If you have experience with God, you will testify how He has led you on a journey to trusting in Him. Those moments when you lose your job, have no money or food to eat, and could not pay the mortgage or electricity bill are the moments when God is shouting, "Will you trust Me now?"

If you did not need a miracle, why would a God of miracles speak to you? If you do, then go through the desert and learn to trust through praise and thanksgiving for who God is for you. Your declaration of faith in the desert will help the Holy Spirit burn from you your desire to complain, blame others, and leave God. If you have little, continue to give to the Lord and to others. If you have little time, continue to serve the Lord and others. Let your sacrifice be evident in times of need that you belong to the Lord. There is glory in the desert because that is the moment of temptation, and also deliverance by the Lord. He will brand the burnt and broken for His purpose. A call to God without affliction is not a call, and our lack of understanding of His ways and His training can sometimes fill us with bitterness that will distort our ministry.

I encourage you to find someone who can speak to you about the reality of faith and trust in God when you only see darkness and want to give up. That place of affliction is a glorious place. It is a place of encounter, birthing a divine vision for you. It is there that you learn to trust God.

Prayer:
Lord, help me identify the things and people around me that I trust more than You. Help me to live a life of repentance, where I learn to trust You more and more. I decide today to put my trust in You. Lord, help me live a life of thanksgiving and praise of You. Lord, refine my heart with Your fire, Your love, and Your Word that my motivations will be pure before You. May Your provision, healing, and deliverance glorify Your name today.

Further Reading

The blessing of the Lord makes rich, and he adds no sorrow with it. Proverbs 10:22

How much better is it to get wisdom than gold! and to get understanding rather to be chosen than silver! Proverbs 16:16

Chapter 4

Faith: A Life Built by God

Now faith is the substance of things hoped for, the evidence of things not seen. Hebrews 11:1

Looking unto Jesus, the author and finisher of our faith, who for the joy that was set before Him endured the cross, despising the shame, and has sat down at the right hand of the throne of God. Hebrews 12:2

Faith is the evidence of things not seen: it is a reality revealed to us. The Lord started the work in you. He *is still working* in you, and He will finish the work if you allow Him. Use challenges as a vehicle for allowing Him to build your faith through your surrender, praise, and worship.

Praise, study, prayer, and declaration of the Word will bring revelations of His plan. Obedience unto Him continues to *build* faith in us. A new reality is built in us that allows us to speak and pray with authority and see miracles happen. If we invest time in seeking God, He will bless us with a new reality through faith. Our trust in Him will increase, and our belief in His ability to do the impossible for our good will increase. Those who have placed their trust in Him through faith carry a testimonial of daily victories won by Him.

God's purpose will then start to unfold in your life as you become a bright light for your community.

Paying attention to the material, size, and purpose of our personal mountains will undermine our faith. When we do so, we start to believe that it is impossible to see any change. We become experts in our own problems and start to enjoy the pain of being a victim. We then develop theologies that lead us far from God, saying that God has favorites and likes to bless other people more than us. That attitude increases our desire to complain and blame God and others for our problems, and it is contagious. We will seek to confirm our negative theology with people who suffer from other problems, contributing to their doubt. Sometimes, we will use scripture to confirm our doubt in God.

Ultimately, it is up to us to choose life or death, and it all starts with the humble attitude of seeking God for forgiveness, deliverance, healing, and purpose. We all start from the same place: one of disbelief and of trusting our jobs, finances, families, and everything else apart from God. The road of true faith is not easy, but it is the only one if you want to follow Jesus Christ. He is the one who will help you to become like Him because He is the author and finisher of your faith.

Our attitude should be pure when sowing the seeds of faith in His kingdom. The work should be done with a heart full of thanks. A desire to share in our tithes and offerings inside and outside the church is just one way that the Lord intervenes in our finances. I urge you to express your faith through your finances. Let your act of giving be an act of public prayer and declaration of your source of blessing—the Lord Jesus Christ. You can pay someone else's bill with your money, but the Lord can give that other person a desire to work and a job to do, thanks to your prayer, making that person a contributor in His kingdom.

Prayer:
Lord, I desire to humble myself before You and surrender all my sin, all my weakness, and all my unbelief. I have spent too much of my life looking at my problems, and doubt has crept into my heart. I surrender

to You once more, and I ask You to create in me a clean heart that will truly worship You and tremble at Your Word. I ask that You circumcise my heart, remove all hindrances, and help me once again to believe. Revive in me the joy of my salvation and help me grow in faith through communion with You. I decide today to follow You and obey at whatever cost. May Your kingdom come, and Your will be done in my life that others will see that I am Your new creation.

Further Reading

> But without faith it is impossible to please Him, for he who comes to God must believe that He is, and that He is a rewarder of those who diligently seek Him. Hebrews 11:6

> And which of you, having a servant plowing or tending sheep, will say to him when he has come in from the field, "Come at once and sit down to eat?" But will he not rather say to him, "Prepare something for my supper, and gird yourself and serve me till I have eaten and drunk, and afterward you will eat and drink?" Does he thank that servant because he did the things that were commanded him? I think not. So likewise you, when you have done all those things which you are commanded, say, "We are unprofitable servants. We have done what was our duty to do." Luke 17:7–10

Chapter 5

Thanksgiving

A way to enter the Lord's presence is the following:

> Enter into His gates with thanksgiving, and into His courts with praise. Be thankful to Him and bless His name. For the Lord is good; His mercy is everlasting, and His truth endures to all generations. Psalm 100:4–5

> Rejoice always, pray without ceasing, in everything give thanks; for this is the will of God in Christ Jesus for you. 1 Thessalonians 5:16–18

We want to enter His presence not only because of what He has done for us but also for how good and loving He is toward us. If you have a relationship with Jesus, it does not matter what you are going through. Nothing of this world can separate you from His love. His love is unconditional and should be the source of our thanksgiving and praise. If you have His love, you have Him. That is why you can do all things through Christ. Provision will be given to those who really want it because it is a provision of purpose before it is a provision of the means to accomplish a purpose. God can work miracles through you, bringing people into freedom without spending a single dollar. Praise is recognizing with your mouth who He is, how good He is, and how great His power is. Whatever your praise, recognize and thank God because He is your first great reward.

Rejoicing is not dependent upon circumstances, nor is thanksgiving. The trials we go through do not disprove God but give God the opportunity to glorify His name and use everything for our good. The good produced is the perfecting of faith that moves mountains. The faith that the Lord brings into our lives becomes a resource in times of need so that we can do good works that point people to the reality of God with us, Jesus Christ.

Jesus's purpose in working the miracle of loaves and fishes was to offer a point of *entrance to reveal the meaning of a relationship with Him through the cross.*

Is that our purpose when we talk to people? Do we really want people to have an encounter with Jesus and know the miracle He worked on the cross? That miracle will bring them healing and deliverance.

> And Jesus took the loaves, and when He had given thanks, He distributed them to the disciples, and the disciples to those sitting down; and likewise of the fish, as much as they wanted. John 6:11

1. He gave thanks for the little they had. Do not despise small beginnings or small offerings because we never know completely the sacrifice and faith behind them.
2. He gave thanks because someone had decided to obey the Lord and give an extravagant offering. A nameless boy may not have been the ideal resource for the miracle to happen. You are not insignificant in the plan of God for provision to happen.
3. He gave thanks because He knew what He was going to do. He gave thanks for God's provision of bread. He gave thanks in faith for what was going to happen.
4. The Word of the Lord was fulfilled as the disciples distributed the bread. The Lord trusted His disciples to give

an offering and give themselves to the distribution of the multiplication to others. That is a kingdom mindset. We assume that the disciples did not starve and also ate, but that was not the point of the miracle.

It is not only our offering but our desire to distribute to others that will produce genuine prayers and actions of faith.

5. Jesus brought His people to a place of isolation because isolation is good for instruction. He wanted to reveal Himself to them as the crucified Christ who would redeem them, but the people were only interested in teaching and natural provision. The provision was the life of this world, the bread, and not eternal life, the life of His world, His living bread. This training was not different from the training that the Israelites went through in the desert after they left Egypt, which shaped them in faith for the mission of God. The Israelites did not want to connect with a god that required them to believe in miracles, but miracles were required to conquer the promised land. They wanted a god to work for them, not to lead them and work through them. That type of self-centeredness had to be ended through trials to a perfect faith in Him who leads us through them. However, the people of God did not want to know Him, to humble themselves, and to let God work in their hearts. That is why in both cases, in the desert in Exodus and the desert with Jesus, the result was a breaking of the fellowship. That is why today, people stop following Jesus because it costs them too much. Provision, therefore, comes from an encounter with the cross that transforms our lives to seek His will and not our own.

Prayer:
Lord, help me become grateful in all circumstances. I want to be grateful for who You are and what You have done for me. I know that you will use everything for my good so I can be refined and shine for you. Everything that happens to me has a purpose in You, and I know that you will

redeem me because of Your mercy and grace. Help me have a grateful heart and praise You.

Further Reading

> Oh, give thanks to the Lord! Call upon His name; Make known His deeds among the peoples! Psalm 105:1

Chapter 6

Joy

But this I say: He who sows sparingly will also reap sparingly, and he who sows bountifully will also reap bountifully. So let each one give as he purposes in his heart, not grudgingly or of necessity; for God loves a cheerful giver. 2 Corinthians 9:6–7

And they spoke to Moses, saying, "The people bring much more than enough for the service of the work which the Lord commanded us to do." Exodus 36:5

Then he said to them, "Go your way, eat the fat, drink the sweet, and send portions to those for whom nothing is prepared; for this day is holy to our Lord. Do not sorrow, for the joy of the Lord is your strength." Nehemiah 8:10

The motivation that leads us to give should be of faith and joy. If we love Jesus, we will obey His commandments. It will not be burdensome to pay the price of following Christ because Christ is worth much more than that. It is only a revelation of the joy of knowing Him that will enable us to give with the right motivation. If you give grudgingly because it is the thing to do or out of necessity, if following Jesus has become a burden, then you need your heart to be restored.

There is a first love that needs to be maintained. It is not a religious routine; it is a lifestyle of devotion to Him. If it is by His mercy that we are saved, and His mercies are new every morning, then it follows that we need to be connected to that fountain of refreshing life that washes our sins away and leads us to repentance. We need to live a lifestyle where the purpose is not us but rather to seek Him and do His will. To do His will is to love Him and your neighbors.

If you pay attention, every day is full of opportunities to pray for people, bless people, listen to people, connect with people, help people, and realize that there are talents and gifts that we have that can set people free. It should fill us with joy to know that really knowing Jesus can help us make Him known. Whatever you do to others in faith will point them to Jesus. Preach the gospel with love and in your actions to the point that they need to ask you about the source of your joy, your motivation, and your purpose. Most people will think that you have a hidden agenda or that you want to sell them something or manipulate them. However, if you are to administer the love of Christ, let it be known that you do not make any requirements. Releasing the Word of God to people and the blessing (perhaps a financial gift or a service they need) is as important as releasing them to the Lord, for you can sow, but only the Lord can bring the increase.

The joy of the Lord should lead us to minister for God and to the people, but it is important to remember that the battle for souls that you are engaged in is won through prayer, fasting, declarations of faith, and mere obedience to the Holy Spirit. You can use any of the gifts He has given you to share God with others. The rest of the work needs to be done by the Holy Spirit. If you pay close attention to Jesus's ministry, you will see that He did not force anyone to have faith. He offered an invitation, and it was the conviction of the Holy Spirit that compelled people to follow Him. May we continue to learn from Him as we work by His side in this harvest.

The joy of giving unto Him is related to a joyful expectation of being called to work in His harvest. The most precious fruits we can bring to Him are souls through the Holy Spirit. To be working with Him at such a great task should fill us with joy.

Prayer:
Lord, give me a revelation of the joy of Your salvation. Help me to obey You and desire to work bountifully for the needs of others. Let it be known to others that my trust, rest, and joy are in the Lord because You are with me, and my help comes from You. Lord, help me and lead me to Your salvation that I may bring other people to repentance and a joyful relationship with You.

Further Reading

> Rejoice in the Lord always. Again I will say, rejoice! Let your gentleness be known to all men. The Lord is at hand. Philippians 4:4–5

> The Lord is my strength and my shield; My heart trusted in Him, and I am helped; Therefore my heart greatly rejoices, and with my song I will praise Him. Psalm 28:7

> Restore to me the joy of Your salvation, and uphold me by Your generous Spirit. Psalm 51:12

> Nevertheless do not rejoice in this, that the spirits are subject to you, but rather rejoice because your names are written in heaven. Luke 10:20

Chapter 7

Contentment

Not that I speak in regard to need, for I have learned in whatever state I am, to be content: I know how to be abased, and I know how to abound. Everywhere and in all things I have learned both to be full and to be hungry, both to abound and to suffer need. I can do all things through Christ who strengthens me. Philippians 4:11–13

But He said to them, "I have food to eat of which you do not know." John 4:32

Though He slay me, yet will I trust Him. Job 13:15

One of the most difficult aspects of following Christ is understanding that once you are positioned with Him to do only His will, other things do not matter. It is impossible to fully accept or agree with Paul's perspective and the perspective of the apostles if we continue to believe that need is necessarily evil and sinful, a position of no faith and no blessing from God. Job was tested to the end, and God saw that his heart was for Him. Paul was also tested in this manner, and even the church of Smyrna (Revelation 2:9) was tested and proven faithful through that trial of poverty. In fact, Jesus saw them as rich because He looked at their work in the kingdom of God.

You may think that contentment is a lack of ambition, no faith in increase, and a lack of purpose. But Paul tells us that he has learned to be content because he has been trained by God to investigate His purpose, no matter what the trial. The final analysis is that Paul can do all things through Christ who is his strength. He has found meat of which the disciples were unaware. Paul, like Jesus before the Samaritan woman, had access to a source of energy that is supernatural. God will go to the extreme to provide strength, health, energy, and everything we get from food, but in a supernatural way.

Therefore, contentment is the right perspective on the possessions entrusted to us for a season. Contentment means having the wisdom to trust God through lack and trusting God for wisdom through abundance as we focus on investing in the kingdom of God. Contentment is the end of the struggle with wanting more from this world, more comfort, more business, more entertainment, more success, more fame, more of everything that the world can give us. When we say, "It is enough in any circumstance," we shift the burden of this life to God. He is the one who will guide us to purpose and increase. An increase may come in many unexpected ways, but it will glorify His name. There will be the Holy Spirit's satisfaction in doing what He has called us to do, and our value system will eventually be revolutionized so we truly care for what He cares for and not only in our free time.

Prayer:
Lord, help me to understand the blessing You have for me so I can enjoy with wisdom and sorrow. Help me to gain a perspective on life that goes beyond what the world seeks. Shape and enlarge my heart to care for the things You care for and remove idols from my heart. May my surrender create a space for Your Holy Spirit to inhabit. Lead me into Your ways of righteousness and peace so that the people I deal with may be blessed. Help me understand and enjoy what You provide and be content in every season. Let me put my trust in Christ once more and let it be known to others that He is my true source of strength.

Further Reading

(Those) who suppose that godliness is a means of gain. From such withdraw yourself. Now godliness with contentment is great gain. For we brought nothing into this world, and it is certain we can carry nothing out. And having food and clothing, with these we shall be content. But those who desire to be rich fall into temptation and a snare, and into many foolish and harmful lusts which drown men in destruction and perdition. For the love of money is a root of all kinds of evil, for which some have strayed from the faith in their greediness, and pierced themselves through with many sorrows. 1 Timothy 6:5–10

If they obey and serve Him, they shall spend their days in prosperity, and their years in pleasures. Job 36:11

The fear of the Lord leads to life, and he who has it will abide in satisfaction; He will not be visited with evil. Proverbs 19:23

And He has said to me, "My grace is sufficient for you, for power is perfected in weakness" Therefore I am well content with weaknesses, with insults, with distresses, with persecutions, with difficulties, for Christ's sake; for when I am weak, then I am strong. 2 Corinthians 12:9–10

Chapter 8

Righteousness

But seek first the kingdom of God and His righteousness, and all these things shall be added to you. Matthew 6:33

And to her it was granted to be arrayed in fine linen, clean and bright, for the fine linen is the righteous acts of the saints. Revelation 19:8

Blessed are those who hunger and thirst for righteousness, for they shall be satisfied. Matthew 5:6

There are forty-five verses in the Bible dealing with righteousness from different perspectives. As with any other subject in the Bible, this topic cannot be worked through with only our own effort. The self has one type of righteousness: self-righteousness. However, Jesus Christ came to save us and make us righteous before our Father. That is why He recognizes the blessedness of those who hunger and thirst for righteousness. These people suffer and engage in fasting and prayer for the sake of righteousness. The promise is firm, and the Lord does not lie. Those who approach Him with that desperation and request will be filled. He looks for people who do that for Him so that He can express His righteousness to the world through them.

In a certain moment, it is also about sharing with people through faith. How much can we reach out to people in the name of the Lord to be a blessing? Job knew about that; he was identified for his righteousness, and he shared with the needy.

It would be erroneous to think that practicing righteousness is just giving alms and receiving from God. The Lord wanted to bless Abraham. He told him, "I am your reward." Jesus spoke to us about how much more God will give through the Holy Spirit to those who ask. Therefore, God's righteousness is imparted by the Holy Spirit so that we can do acts of righteousness. Everything takes a special meaning if it is done in the name of the Lord. That means that our trust in God is so great that we believe God will endorse and confirm those acts as His. Jesus worked signs and wonders, and He wants us to work in the same way. Our righteousness should be a sign leading to Him. In fact, He often wants to intervene so that people will have an encounter with Him.

There are two examples that help us understand the connection between God's power and the poor. Peter and John could not meet the financial needs of the lame but went beyond to bring the individual into full healing and restoration through God. The Lord delights when we help the poor, and He also delights when we bring the poor into a relationship with Him that will deliver them from their chains. His kingdom manifested through us is a kingdom of mercy and power.

Prayer:
Lord, help me not only to understand righteousness but also to walk in righteousness. May my life bring life to those around me and in many other nations. May my sacrifice for the wellbeing of Your people be remembered before You that You will reach out with Your hand and bring salvation to many. Help me, Lord, to distribute Your wealth by faith that it will cause people not only to be fed but also to raise up in faith to leap, jump, and praise You, leaving their spiritual lameness behind.

Further Reading

Take heed that you do not do your charitable deeds before men, to be seen by them. Otherwise you have no reward from your Father in heaven. Therefore, when you do a charitable deed, do not sound a trumpet before you as the hypocrites do in the synagogues and in the streets, that they may have glory from men. Assuredly, I say to you, they have their reward. Matthew 6:1–2

I will greatly rejoice in the Lord, my soul shall be joyful in my God; for He has clothed me with the garments of salvation, He has covered me with the robe of righteousness, as a bridegroom decks himself with ornaments, and as a bride adorns herself with her jewels. Isaiah 61:10

He has shown you, O man, what is good; And what does the Lord require of you but to do justly, to love mercy, and to walk humbly with your God? Micah 6:8

Seek the Lord while He may be found, call upon Him while He is near. Isaiah 55:6

I traverse the way of righteousness, in the midst of the paths of justice, that I may cause those who love me to inherit wealth, that I may fill their treasuries. Proverbs 8:20–21

Chapter 9

Fear of the Lord and Tithing

The fear of the Lord is the beginning of knowledge, but fools despise wisdom and instruction. Proverbs 1:7

And you shall eat before the LORD your God, in the place where He chooses to make His name abide, the tithe of your grain and your new wine and your oil, of the firstborn of your herds and your flocks, that you may learn to *fear the LORD* your God always. Deuteronomy 14:23

At the end of *every* third year, you shall bring out the tithe of your produce of that year and store *it* up within your gates. And the Levite, because he has no portion nor inheritance with you, and the stranger and the fatherless and the widow who *are* within your gates, may come and eat and be satisfied, that the lord your God may bless you in all the work of your hand which you do. Deuteronomy 14:28–29

Both Deuteronomy 14 and 18 bring together the concept of preparation in the fear of the Lord through obedience, managing well the abundance that He gives to the people of Israel. The trials and tribulations that the people of Israel suffered were precisely to help them refocus their desires and motivations from a desire for Egypt to a desire to know and worship God. Moses had many years of his own, training in the desert before God called him. However, it was difficult for the people of Israel to learn, to humble themselves, and to prepare for that encounter with the fear of the Lord on the mountain (Exodus 19). It was because they did not learn to fear the Lord that they were filled with terror. Being thankful through trials and tribulations in the desert and preparing themselves for an encounter with the Lord would have changed their faith perspective, allowing them to conquer the promised land by the power of God. If they had feared the Lord, they would have received God's wisdom and known what to do in those moments when they were tested.

I seriously suggest study and pray for knowledge of the fear of God. It will keep you on the right path and help you manage the abundance that God will pour into your life. The Lord is satisfied with your obedience to Him and your generosity unto others. Deuteronomy 18 clearly states that we should share with people in our community who struggle but who we do not know. A possible application of this would be to engage with a local NGO that assists people on the fringes of society, those who find it difficult to get help.

Over the last eight years, I have been involved with a local charity called Project Unity in Bryan, Texas. My first approach was mainly prayer and donations. I asked the president of the institution to meet with me and pray over the check I gave her, trusting in the Lord for His supernatural provision. She told me afterward that the Lord had provided. My main objective in this relationship was to represent the church as an agent to bless the community. I have supervised visits among imprisoned parents and their children, HIV patients, and other groups in need in our city.

The fear of the Lord is devotion and obedience to His Word. The Lord says in Deuteronomy 8 that there is a blessing for those who worship Him and no other gods. May we receive a revelation today of what it means to worship Him only so that we may take up His purpose and receive His provision.

Prayer:

Lord, I ask You for an experiential revelation of the spirit and fear of the Lord. Cleanse my heart so that I can clearly hear You and obey You. May my life be an offering unto You as I seek to do Your will. Deliver me from all temptation and empower me to bless other people in Your name. I ask You for the wisdom to manage the amazing wealth that You bring to me. One dollar that You use to bring someone to Your salvation will bring me joy. I thank You that You have chosen me to do this work and finance the kingdom.

Further Reading

> But on this one will I look: on him who is poor and of a contrite spirit, and who trembles at My word. Isaiah 66:2

> Your word I have hidden in my heart, That I might not sin against You. Psalm 119:11

> Therefore you shall keep the commandments of the LORD your God, to walk in His ways and *to fear Him.* For the LORD your God is bringing you into a good land, a land of brooks of water, of fountains and springs, that flow out of valleys and hills; a land of wheat and barley, of vines and fig trees and pomegranates, a land of olive oil and honey; a land in which you will eat bread without scarcity, in which you will lack nothing; a land whose stones *are* iron and out of whose hills you can dig copper. When you have eaten and are full, *then you shall bless* the LORD your God for the good land which He has given you. Deuteronomy 8:6–10

> And you shall remember the LORD your God, for *it is* He who gives *you power to get wealth,* that

He may *establish His covenant which* He swore to your fathers, as *it is* this day. Then it shall be, if you by any means forget the LORD your God, and follow other gods, and serve them and worship them, I testify against you this day that you shall surely perish. As the nations which the LORD destroys before you, so you shall perish, because you would not be obedient to the voice of the LORD your God. Deuteronomy 8:18–20

Chapter 10

The Power of Sacrifice

So they cried aloud, and cut themselves, as was
their custom, with knives and lances, until the
blood gushed out on them. 1 Kings 18:28

I have been crucified with Christ; it is no longer
I who live, but Christ lives in me; and the life
which I now live in the flesh I live by faith in the
Son of God, who loved me and gave Himself for
me. Galatians 2:20

So when they had eaten breakfast, Jesus said to
Simon Peter, "Simon, son of Jonah, do you love
Me more than these?" He said to Him, "Yes,
Lord; You know that I love You." He said to him,
"Feed My lambs." John 21:15

In Kings 18, we see how people who were worshipping demonic
spirits obtained their power. They danced, worshipped that spirit, and
sacrificed to it by cutting themselves. There was a sacrifice involved
that engaged the spirit to release a response. We have the ability to
bring a response from heaven, but we need to understand what part
of heaven will respond. If we submit to God and worship, we engage
God to release a response on our behalf. If you seek only His king-

dom, you must sacrifice seeking other kingdoms and possessions, but things will be added to you. The only obstacle facing us is awakening to that truth (by having a revelation) and expressing obedience (i.e., paying the price in faith).

Jesus spent time with the disciples, training them not to look for things in this world such as power, reputation, and material wealth, but rather to seek God and do His will. This required acceptance and a changed mindset regarding the consequences (in that Christ would be crucified). They had to commit their lives to God so that they would not fear death. After Peter's denial, he went back to fishing. He may have thought that Jesus had not succeeded in making him a disciple, and it was time to go back to his job. However, Jesus restored him through another financial miracle and invited him into a loving relationship.

John 21 tells us how Jesus invited Peter to serve Him through ministry to others, feeding His lambs. Even though we sometimes do not feel qualified to minister unto others, there are always gifts and blessings that we can share in faith. If you want to sacrifice to the Lord, do not make it only through tithes and offerings. Include every talent that you have. Can you fix someone's car? Cook a meal for someone? Pray for someone in the hospital? Endorse a business that has blessed you? Share the jewelry you have designed? Teach someone how to remove the weeds from their garden? Clean a toilet? Pray and share an encouraging word? There are thousands of ways that you can be a blessing to the church and the people around you. If you read Romans 12, you will see that your service, a living sacrifice, includes all acts of service unto God.

You may think, *If I only take care of others, who will take care of me?* The act of complete selflessness unto God in sacrifice and faith will release something from heaven. You will experience the scripture where it says that it is more blessed to give than to receive. Other people will come to help you, and the Lord will produce miracles around you that will amaze you. However, the greatest miracle is that you will deeply appreciate what comes to you from the Lord, without a sense of entitlement or selfishness. It will be quite easy for you to share what you get because you will know that it was never yours. It was a blessing from the Lord. The right perspective will bring the appreciation of and wisdom regarding what to do with the blessing that you receive

Jesus came to serve, and He sends His people to serve. His objective is eternity by pleasing the Father. His objective for you is to make you a disciple through restoration. Your failure is not big enough to separate you from Him. He wants to restore you to His service.

Prayer/declaration:

Father, I recognize that I have invested so much time in the wrong places. I pray that You will cause my spirit to awaken and take hold of Your Word. Your Word is truth, and it will set me free. Help me to obey by paying the price of discipleship. Remove all fear of lack and desire for self-gratification. I desire to see other people prosper. Lead me to bless people by faith and see them experience miracles in their families, finances, and jobs. Father, give me ideas on how to bless my brothers, sisters, and friends in creative ways that will meet their needs. I pray that as I bless them, You will also bless them in the spirit by setting them free and giving them the revelation of who You are as our Father.

Further Reading

> Knowing that you were not redeemed with corruptible things, like silver or gold, from your aimless conduct received by tradition from your fathers, but with the precious blood of Christ, as of a lamb without blemish and without spot. 1 Peter 1:18–19

> But if the Spirit of Him who raised Jesus from the dead dwells in you, He who raised Christ from the dead will also give life to your mortal bodies through His Spirit who dwells in you. Romans 8:11

> They immediately left their nets and followed Him. Matthew 4:20

Then Jesus said to His disciples, "If anyone desires to come after Me, let him deny himself, and take up his cross, and follow Me." Matthew 16:24

I beseech you therefore, brethren, by the mercies of God, that you present your bodies a living sacrifice, holy, acceptable to God, which is your reasonable service. Romans 12:1

Chapter 11

A Unified Sacrifice Will Bring the Harvest

"Now is the judgment of this world; now the ruler of this world will be cast out. And I, if I am lifted up from the earth, will draw all *peoples* to Myself." This He said, signifying by what death He would die. John 12:31–32

I have been crucified with Christ; it is no longer I who live, but Christ lives in me; and the life which I now live in the flesh I live by faith in the Son of God, who loved me and gave Himself for me. Galatians 2:20

I pray that they will all be one, just as You and I are one—as you are in me, Father, and I am in You. And may they be in us so that the world will believe You sent me. John 17:21

And he said to Him, "Lord, You know all things; You know that I love You." Jesus said to him, "Feed My sheep." John 21:17

The power of the cross is not only found in what Jesus did for us but also revealed to us when we allow the Holy Spirit to do the work of the cross in us. The cross becomes a place of encounter and death that calls for the resurrection of life in His Spirit. To completely surrender to Christ is to allow Him to put to death all our dead works, our works of the flesh, and our sinful tendencies and appetites and to awaken a desire and hunger to seek the Lord, His kingdom, and His righteousness.

We need to believe that there is now a time when God has given us access to Him. Through the blood and body of Jesus Christ, we receive from Him (Hebrews 10:19–25) what we need for this life that His name be glorified in us. His glorification comes as our lives conform to the image of Jesus (Romans 8:29). This enables people to see in us the love, mercy, grace, and power God displays through our lives.

There is a hidden promise in John 12 and 21. The promise is that the Lord will give us sheep to feed. Our faith needs to increase through our knowledge and expectation of a harvest. The revelation that we need to accept, wait for, and experience is this. When Jesus died on the cross, He began waiting for people to come to Him as living sacrifices, manifesting the same release of power. It is because we lose our lives that we gain His (Matthew 10:39). As Paul says, if we die with Him, the Holy Spirit will start drawing people to us to see the life of Christ in us. When Jesus said, "I will draw all peoples," He was also prophesying about a church that would touch nations. We need to be a part of that church and allow the Holy Spirit to bring the conviction and revelation of Christ through us. It is a promise given to us in Christ. The Lord adds to the church daily (Acts 2:47). Let us engage with Him again in true submission and honor Him.

I encourage you to seek unity in the Spirit (Ephesians 4:3) and love in order to fulfill Jesus's prayer in John 17:21. The Father wants to answer that prayer through us as we work together for Him. The result is the harvest. People will come to believe in Jesus. Jesus sent Peter into the deep, but he had to ask for help and work together with people to bring the great multitude of fish ashore. Let's also be prepared to bring them to be a part of our fellowship and the church together.

We need to decide to commit ourselves to the work of the kingdom, seeking God in prayer through His Word, and being leaders of many unto salvation in service, action, and power. That was the work that the Lord gave the apostles, and He is entrusting us once more with that work today.

Prayer:
Lord, help me believe and receive every promise you have for me in Christ. I surrender all, and I accept the apostolic call that is upon Christ and His church to touch nations. I pray that You will help me completely surrender and submit to Your Word and that the Holy Spirit will draw souls to me to be saved and discipled. I pray that You will finish the work of faith in me and make my life fruitful so that it may touch nations and generations for Your glory and for Your name.

Further Reading

> Then with the stones he built an altar in the name of the Lord; and he made a trench around the altar large enough to hold two seahs of seed. And he put the wood in order, cut the bull in pieces, and laid it on the wood, and said, "Fill four waterpots with water, and pour it on the burnt sacrifice and on the wood." Then he said, "Do it a second time," and they did it a second time; and he said, "Do it a third time," and they did it a third time. So the water ran all around the altar; and he also filled the trench with water. And it came to pass, at the time of the offering of the evening sacrifice. 1 Kings 18:32–36

> Then the fire of the Lord fell and consumed the burnt sacrifice, and the wood and the stones and the dust, and it licked up the water that was in the trench. Now when all the people saw it, they

fell on their faces; and they said, "The Lord, He is God! The Lord, He is God!" 1 Kings 18:38–39

But he is a Jew who is one inwardly; and circumcision is that of the heart, in the Spirit, not in the letter; whose praise is not from men but from God. Romans 2:29

I will give you a new heart and put a new spirit within you; I will take the heart of stone out of your flesh and give you a heart of flesh. I will put My Spirit within you and cause you to walk in My statutes, and you will keep My judgments and do them. Ezekiel 36:26–27

He who has My commandments and keeps them, it is he who loves Me. And he who loves Me will be loved by My Father, and I will love him and manifest Myself to him." John 14:21

After these things I looked, and behold, a great multitude which no one could number, of all nations, tribes, peoples, and tongues, standing before the throne and before the Lamb, clothed with white robes, with palm branches in their hands. Revelation 7:9

Section II

Unique Figures in the Kingdom's Purpose: Learning from the Best

In this section, we explore aspects of the lives of Abraham, Joseph, Moses, Daniel, and Paul. We consider important life moments that shaped the futures of those leaders of the faith. They all obeyed God and made drastic declarations and changes in their lives, showing their commitment to Him. Abraham left his father's house in great expectation of God giving him land. Joseph was sent away from his father's house without any desire for revenge. Moses led Israel out of Egypt even though he felt the least qualified to do it. Daniel set himself apart and challenged the diet provided in Babylon because his God commanded him to do so. Finally, Paul remained hidden, seeking the Lord and risking his life for the gospel, sharing a message he had previously tried to stop by persecuting Christians. They all had high and low moments when they had to trust the Lord to survive.

It is my prayer that you will be challenged to read the Bible to seek and find new treasures from the lives of these heroes of faith. I believe the Lord will show you more and challenge you to trust Him to perfect your faith. I declare that your eyes will be opened to look beyond, and you will find themes and points of connection in the lives of those men who showed a deep love and trust in God, regardless of their situations. Those lives are an example of Job's declaration: "Though He slay me, yet will I trust Him" (Job 13:15).

I suggest you consider the whole journey that is communicated to us through the scriptures. There is a training program of faith that God uses to reveal His ways to His people. May the Lord guide you prophetically in this season so that you can take the necessary steps to establish the foundation for the plan He has for your future. It is essential that we embrace a time of preparation and consecration for that to happen. Even though the path to salvation is narrow and uncomfortable, it is full of fruit for others and will lead you to your harvest.

Chapter 12

Abraham

Now the Lord had said to Abram: "Get out of your country, from your family, and from your father's house, to a land that I will show you. I will make you a great nation." Genesis 12:1–2

And behold, the word of the Lord came to him, saying, "This one shall not be your heir, but one who will come from your own body shall be your heir." Then He brought him outside and said, "Look now toward heaven, and count the stars if you are able to number them." And He said to him, "So shall your descendants be." And he believed in the Lord, and He accounted it to him for righteousness. Genesis 15:4–6

No longer shall your name be called Abram, but your name shall be Abraham; for I have made you a father of many nations. Genesis 17:5

And He said, "Do not lay your hand on the lad, or do anything to him; for now I know that you fear God, since you have not withheld your son, your only son, from Me." Genesis 22:12

And Abraham called the name of the place, The-Lord-Will-Provide; as it is said to this day, "In the Mount of the Lord it shall be provided." Genesis 22:14

Abraham is a unique example of the faith-building process that God uses to inspire us to become His provider. The Lord sees Abraham's heart and leads him to sacrifice. This happens several times, and every time the Lord calls him, it is because He wants to release a promise over his life. The Lord leads him to a new land and trains him to trust Him for deliverance against attack and protection from the Egyptians. From the moment Abraham leaves his father's house and enters God's will, the Lord provides for him in different ways. However, the narrative in the book of Genesis rarely deals with material provision, except in times of famine. More often, it addresses the supernatural provision of God's purpose.

We know that Abraham made mistakes. He went to Egypt when God could have guided him elsewhere for provision. In Egypt, he went in the wrong direction by trying to help God fulfill His promise of a son. He had a second wife and son. Ishmael was not God's promise. That was Abraham trying to help God. It took Abraham a long while to give up his dream of making Ishmael his heir, but God's grace abounded at every moment because Abraham was learning to believe in God in that foreign land.

It took a long time for Abraham to be trained. This is because the Lord wanted to teach him many things. Isaac was a miracle son who came at an age when couples are normally unable to have children. Isaac was God's provision not only in response to Abraham's request but also in response to God's request. You can follow that development in Genesis 22. Throughout all of that time, God was training Abraham to believe in Him and the fulfillment of His Word. It took a long time, but it was necessary for that type of faith to be born in Abraham's heart. God did not give Abraham faith to believe only in Isaac's birth. He gave him faith to believe in the resurrection.

When it was time to sacrifice Isaac, Abraham was asked to kill any emotional attachment to God's blessing. He was asked to put to death something inside of him. Both Abraham and Isaac came down from that mountain, knowing God to be the provider of eternal life. At the same time, Abraham knew at that moment that God had finished some work in him. God had fulfilled His purpose for Abraham. It was at that moment that Abraham received the revelation of God as a provider and the fulfillment of His Word in his life, at whatever cost.

From God's perspective, something had been achieved that would touch generations. The promise that God made to Abraham is remarkably similar to the promise of Jesus to His church. He declares his family victorious over the enemy. Those points of influence, those gates, are conquered in Jesus's name so that the name of the Lord will be glorified. My prayer for you is that you will not limit God to being just a provider of your daily needs but that you will equip yourself to accept every good work in the spirit. He will provide His kingdom and purpose for you.

Prayer:
Father, help me see Your kingdom. Help me receive Your kingdom. Help me do Your will on earth. I surrender my reliance on material things before You, and I ask that You transform my heart such that I may focus on revealing Christ to others, and generations will come to be blessed. I thank You for Your supernatural provision, and I praise You for Your love and will to bless me with Yourself.

Further Reading

> Blessing I will bless you, and multiplying I will multiply your descendants as the stars of the heaven and as the sand which is on the seashore; and your descendants shall possess the gate of their enemies. In your seed all the nations of the earth shall be blessed, because you have obeyed My voice. Genesis 22:17–18

And I also say to you that you are Peter, and on this rock I will build My church, and the gates of Hades shall not prevail against it. Matthew 16:18

Chapter 13

Joseph

Now Joseph had a dream. Genesis 37:5

Then he dreamed still another dream. Genesis 37:9

The Lord was with Joseph, and he was a successful man. Genesis 39:2

So it was, from the time that he had made him overseer of his house and all that he had, that the Lord blessed the Egyptian's house for Joseph's sake. Genesis 39:5

The keeper of the prison did not look into anything that was under Joseph's authority, because the Lord was with him; and whatever he did, the Lord made it prosper. Genesis 39:23

What is your dream? Has the Lord given you one? Have you asked the Lord for one? Genesis 37 tells us that Joseph got into trouble with his brothers and endured slavery because he had a dream. We have grown to despise the process with which the Lord brings us to our purpose, but that was not in Joseph's heart. That dream that cost him so much was the same dream that kept him going. It was the purity of his heart obtained through trials that attracted the presence of God. He knew the Lord was with him because it was evident in the blessing he brought to others through his service.

Some people define a blessing as God's direct provision to them, but Joseph could see God's blessing within the blessings of others. God's sign to him was training him to hold a position of authority wherever he went. That was the initial dream—authority over his family—a blessing even though his family could not understand it. However, the dream was even bigger!

Do you have a dream? Well, make it bigger because the Lord will surprise you! God's dream for Joseph was of deliverance and blessing toward his own family. He received that revelation when famine came. When famine appears, your family will come to those who have been trained by the Lord. We know that the Lord gave Joseph a position of great authority in Egypt so that his influence could preserve life. Joseph's actions became an ark within which people could find protection against famine and destruction.

Have you been through God's process of provision? In my experience, everyone must choose to go through it. We know that faith is built through adversity by trusting the Lord, but it is adversity that also invites us to draw far from God. However, if you connect deeply to your dream, invest yourself in that dream, and humble yourself before God, then God will use those same circumstances to speak to you, to tell you that the Lord is with you and that you are doing His work. The Lord will cause people around you to be blessed, and, in turn, the blessing will touch you.

Have you realized that God has a bigger purpose for you than what you can see? He wants to make you strong and use you to turn people back to Him. In Zechariah 12, the Lord says that on that day, the feeblest will be like David. God's intention is to make His whole church strong and not only a few. His church will be displayed as a blessing to others. Remember that many seeds are sown during unexpected times. When you show strength and faith in adversity, you speak a loud message in the spirit that people will receive. The Holy Spirit will bring a joyful harvest to those who have sown in tears.

Prayer:
Lord, help me see, help me dream, and help me discern the plans you have for me. Even though I cannot see everything, I know that the time will come when You will show me, and it is my faith and hope that, as I walk in faith and know You, You will strengthen me and show me the work to do, the cities to influence, and the nations to impact. I pray for wisdom to manage the task at hand, for humility to relate without prejudice to the lost, and for Your love to be displayed through my life.

Further Reading

> Then it came to pass, at the end of two full years, that Pharaoh had a dream. Genesis 41:1

> And Pharaoh said to his servants, "Can we find such a one as this, a man in whom is the Spirit of God?" Genesis 41:38

> And Pharaoh said to Joseph, "See, I have set you over all the land of Egypt." Genesis 41:41

> And God sent me before you to preserve a posterity for you in the earth, and to save your lives by a great deliverance. So now it was not you who sent me here, but God; and He has made me a father to Pharaoh, and Lord of all his house, and a ruler throughout all the land of Egypt. Genesis 45:7–8

Chapter 14

Moses

Come now, therefore, and I will send you to Pharaoh that you may bring My people, the children of Israel, out of Egypt. But Moses said to God, "Who am I that I should go to Pharaoh, and that I should bring the children of Israel out of Egypt?" Exodus 3:10–11

"The Lord God of the Hebrews has met with us; and now, please, let us go three days" journey into the wilderness, that we may sacrifice to the Lord our God. Exodus 3:18

But every woman shall ask of her neighbor, namely, of her who dwells near her house, articles of silver, articles of gold, and clothing; and you shall put them on your sons and on your daughters. So you shall plunder the Egyptians." Exodus 3:22

The same way Joseph was trained for his job, Moses had to spend many years in the wilderness to prepare to meet with God. The person most favored in Egypt lost all of his confidence, struggling to talk with and obey God. Notice that God does not give up on us despite our many failures. He still wants to redeem us and prepare us for His work.

Even though God was clear with Moses, the message was not received; there was no hunger and thirst for God. The Israelites' desire was more for deliverance than to meet with God. They desired to obey the Lord and leave Egypt, but in their hearts, they were not ready to obey Moses. The Lord speaks about the importance of spiritual leadership. Moses was God's vehicle of deliverance and provision but not accepted for his position with God, only for his ability to work miracles for their benefit.

The Israelites' lack of consecration hindered them from meeting with the Lord, and because they could not overcome their fleshly desires, their need led them to idol worship and the creation of the golden calf. These Christians wanted to enter their promised land, but they had not learned to consecrate themselves and worship God. It is a life of worshipping the Lord in spirit and truth that leads to victory. However, they were still moved by a god they worshipped, a god they created with money that allowed them the pleasures of the world. Philippians 3:19 conveyed it as such: "Their destiny is destruction, their god is their stomach, and their glory is in their shame. Their mind is set on earthly things."

However, Moses did not give up and fulfilled one of his most delicate tasks. He began to intercede for the fallen people, people who did not have the desire to meet God or wait for God, people who were disconnected from God. One of the roles of the Christian royal priesthood is to intercede on behalf of the land. In the same way we worship God and intercede together, there were great victories by Joshua and other people the Lord sent to fight battles. Intercession is very often a neglected work in the church; however, if you want to fulfill the call of God, you will need to stand in the gap. There will be people who the Lord will entrust to you. God will entrust His victory to true worshippers and intercessors. He will ensure that they are prosperous in every area of their lives.

Prayer:

Lord, make me a worshipper and an intercessor. Help me to consecrate myself before You and seek You with all my heart. I desire to know You and to make You known. I pray that You will give me discernment and the conviction to leave behind all hindrance, all unbelief, and all sin that separate me from You. I thank You for wanting to lift me so that people will know that You have sent me to them.

Further Reading

> And so it was, when Moses held up his hand, that Israel prevailed; and when he let down his hand, Amalek prevailed. But Moses' hands became heavy; so they took a stone and put it under him, and he sat on it. And Aaron and Hur supported his hands, one on one side, and the other on the other side; and his hands were steady until the going down of the sun. So Joshua defeated Amalek and his people with the edge of the sword. Exodus 17:11–13

> And he received the gold from their hand, and he fashioned it with an engraving tool, and made a molded calf. Then they said, "This is your god, O Israel, that brought you out of the land of Egypt!" So when Aaron saw it, he built an altar before it. And Aaron made a proclamation and said, "Tomorrow is a feast to the Lord." Then they rose early on the next day, offered burnt offerings, and brought peace offerings; and the people sat down to eat and drink, and rose up to play. Exodus 32:4–6

> [Moses interceded with the Lord.] Turn from Your fierce wrath, and relent from this harm to Your people. Remember Abraham, Isaac, and

Israel, Your servants, to whom You swore by Your own self, and said to them, "I will multiply your descendants as the stars of heaven; and all this land that I have spoken of I give to your descendants, and they shall inherit it forever." So the Lord relented from the harm which He said He would do to His people. Exodus 32:12–14

So the Lord said to Moses: "See, I have made you as God to Pharaoh, and Aaron your brother shall be your prophet." Exodus 7:1

Chapter 15

Daniel

But Daniel purposed in his heart that he would not defile himself with the portion of the king's delicacies, nor with the wine which he drank; therefore he requested of the chief of the eunuchs that he might not defile himself. Daniel 1:8

As for these four young men, God gave them knowledge and skill in all literature and wisdom; and Daniel had understanding in all visions and dreams. Daniel 1:17

Then the king interviewed them, and among them all none was found like Daniel, Hananiah, Mishael, and Azariah; therefore, they served before the king. And in all matters of wisdom and understanding about which the king examined them, he found them ten times better than all the magicians and astrologers who were in all his realm. Daniel 1:19–20

Daniel and his friends decided to be the only Jews in Babylon to honor God by keeping His word regarding the types of food that they should eat (Leviticus 11:4–20). This leap of faith to refuse food from Babylon could have been seen as an insult. However, Daniel and his friends trusted God for deliverance at that time, and in the end, they received much more.

Daniel's separation could also have engendered scorn and contempt in other Jews who had decided to be more open to the new culture. We don't know about that, but we do know about a triple miracle that they received that gave them advancement in their position and consequently the financial reward they received. Yes, I am assuming that the king sometimes financially rewarded those who served him. The first miracle was that after those ten days of vegetable fasting, the Lord made them more energetic and healthier than the rest when the eunuch's expectation was a different outcome. The second miracle was that God gave them knowledge and wisdom. They had been prepared by God to pass the king's test. Finally, the third miracle was a supernatural gift given to Daniel—his ability to understand visions and dreams.

We see in the following chapters that Daniel's gift, together with his discipline of intercession, gave him the ability to address the many challenges that came to him. God had given him a supernatural way to be successful in his job. But what is the real lesson here? And what is the actual application for us? We learn extremely hard lessons from Daniel, but we need to learn from his testimony if we want to shine in this hour.

First, he showed us that sacrifice unto God through fasting and prayer was part of his way of separation. A more basic principle is that complete obedience to the Word of God, even when amid disobedience, is required if we want to be separated unto God. It is only a pure heart, a heart that loves God that will be willing to pay the price of separation unto Him. This is because this type of heart is of strong conviction and very discerning on issues regarding sin.

The second essential lesson that we learn from Daniel's life is that God will always give us more than we expect. There will be a provision of natural and supernatural gifts to you so that you might do your future job. God wants to train you, but do you really want to be trained for His service?

The third essential lesson is that the work that God will call you to do may not be only in the church but also in the marketplace or politics. One thing is certain. There will be a place of authority and a way to lead people into salvation. I pray that reading this chapter will lead you to read the book of Daniel prayerfully and see these miracles at work. Daniel used his spiritual gift of dreams and visions many times. It helped him not only solve problems for the king but also receive prophetic words for future generations.

There is one more lesson that preparation brings. It releases the grace and discernment not to bow down to foreign gods. Daniel faced lions, and his friends were thrown into a furnace, but they did not flinch. They could not die because they were already dead to this world and lived only unto God; therefore, God delivered them. A moment that could have marked complete defeat turned out to be the point of complete victory and promotion. Consecration unto God is not devoid of challenges, but if you embrace those by faith, there is a testimony, promotion, and harvest on the other side. You will be transformed, and know that only transformed people can transform people.

Prayer:
Lord, I surrender to You. Give me complete discernment and conviction regarding sin. Help me consecrate myself before You and choose to obey You whatever the price. I seek Your face and Your hand to train me and empower me to do Your will. I pray for the harvest when You will bring forth Your glory. Help me be prepared to overcome times of testing, for I believe in Your great deliverance.

Further Reading

> Nebuchadnezzar spoke, saying, "Blessed be the God of Shadrach, Meshach, and Abed-Nego, who sent His Angel and delivered His servants who trusted in Him, and they have frustrated the king's word, and yielded their bodies, that they should not serve nor worship any god except

their own God! Therefore I make a decree that any people, nation, or language which speaks anything amiss against the God of Shadrach, Meshach, and Abed-Nego shall be cut in pieces, and their houses shall be made an ash heap; because there is no other God who can deliver like this." Daniel 3:28–29

I make a decree that in every dominion of my kingdom men must tremble and fear before the God of Daniel. For He is the living God, and steadfast forever; His kingdom is the one which shall not be destroyed, and His dominion shall endure to the end. He delivers and rescues, and He works signs and wonders in heaven and on earth, who has delivered Daniel from the power of the lions. So this Daniel prospered in the reign of Darius and in the reign of Cyrus the Persian. Daniel 6:26–28

Chapter 16

Paul

For the love of money is a root of all kinds of evil, for which some have strayed from the faith in their greediness and pierced themselves through with many sorrows. 1 Timothy 6:10

So we urged Titus, that as he had begun, so he would also complete this grace in you as well. But as you abound in everything—in faith, in speech, in knowledge, in all diligence, and in your love for us—see that you abound in this grace also. 2 Corinthians 8:6–7

Let him who stole steal no longer, but rather let him labor, working with his hands what is good, that he may have something to give him who has need. Ephesians 4:28

For I am already being poured out as a drink offering, and the time of my departure is at hand. I have fought the good fight, I have finished the race, I have kept the faith. Finally, there is laid up for me the crown of righteousness, which the Lord, the righteous Judge, will give to me on that

Day, and not to me only but also to all who have
loved His appearing. 2 Timothy 4:6–8

Paul teaches us many things about our relationship with money, sowing, and other related topics. He gives practical advice, urging us to invest our time living by faith in God and doing good works.

Contrary to the belief of many, money is *not* the root of all evil, but the love of money is. In fact, it is so dangerous that it leads people far from faith and into greed, selfish ambition, and many other sins. The main challenge we have here is conviction regarding sin. We live in a world that worships money, but many people are not aware of that. In my opinion, people who have consecrated their finances to God and allow Him to do deep work in their hearts have no problem giving to others and are very sensitive to the guidance of the Holy Spirit. As they follow Jesus, He leads them to sow their talent, time, and treasure into many areas through faith. It is a river that keeps giving for other people to enjoy. However, many other people are still waiting to hear what the new formula is that will give the least so that they can have the most from God. They reduce God to a type of divine banker willing to finance their flesh-created plans. They have made money their God and God their slave.

Paul tells us in 2 Corinthians 8 that sowing an apostolic call is a grace from God. Titus was charged to teach and impart that grace. In this sense, grace is defined as the supernatural ability given by God to do supernatural sowing, with an expectation that God will move through that act of partnership in the kingdom. Paul teaches us that willing hearts can receive the ability to do this type of work if led by the Holy Spirit. This is vastly different from Titus trying to persuade or manipulate the Corinthians with empty marketing messages and false promises to have compassion on a starving Paul.

Paul encouraged people to work so that they could earn an income, with the objective of having more than enough to share. In this sense, our jobs are a means to bless people, first by working in jobs that bring value to people. Laziness is not an act of faith. Proverbs 10:4 tells us that "lazy hands make for poverty, but diligent hands bring wealth." The main point is that in at least two different ways, work is a sacred activity unto the Lord, done for the benefit of others. A company creates value through the services it sells to customers. It also creates wealth to be shared, and if you are generous, you can create a corporate social responsibility strategy where profits from your business can be sown by faith to the development of others.

One of the many points of revelation that Paul taught is the giving of ourselves to the Lord and others, with a desire to finish the race well and with the expectation of a reward, a crown for those who work for His kingdom and who passionately love His presence and the work He accomplished on the cross. It is because Paul paid a high price at that time, being jailed, flogged, and beaten for the gospel that he had complete discernment about his eternal reward. It is my prayer that we will all have the same mindset and desire to love Jesus so that we invest our lives in Him and for Him. Paul knew that the price he paid created a glory in Him to bless others. He was not selfish. His life in Christ was a commitment to bring the gospel to the lost and to form churches.

Prayer:

Lord, I pray that You open my eyes to see my true condition regarding money and Your kingdom. Give me the faith and grace to sow and become a constant sower. Let it be my lifestyle that I share with others in Your name. Help me get back on track because I want to finish this race well. I want to desire eternal rewards and let my life and death count for the restoration of Your glory on earth.

Further Reading

> Command those who are rich in this present age not to be haughty, nor to trust in uncertain riches but in the living God, who gives us richly all things to enjoy. Let them do good, that they be rich in good works, ready to give, willing to share, storing up for themselves a good founda-

tion for the time to come, that they may lay hold on eternal life. 1 Timothy 6:17–19

But this I say: He who sows sparingly will also reap sparingly, and he who sows bountifully will also reap bountifully. 2 Corinthians 9:6

And my God shall supply all your need according to His riches in glory by Christ Jesus. Philippians 4:19

Section III

Essential Aspects of Kingdom Discovery

The purpose of this section is to ignite a hunger to know God, the Father, Son, and Holy Spirit. We need a revelation regarding the purpose of the church. This is a lifelong challenge that will take everything we have.

At one point in his life, Simon and some of his colleagues left everything to follow Jesus (Luke 5:11). As they learned from Jesus, Peter reminded him of this sacrifice (Matthew 19:27, Luke 18:28). Jesus answered that there is a reward on earth and in the age to come. John also spoke of the moment where the disciples were tempted to join the crowd and leave Jesus (John 6:68), but Peter confessed that Jesus had the Word of eternal life, which was what he needed. Following God has always required much (Hebrews 11), and Jesus has also clearly declared the price of discipleship (Matthew 10:39).

Since the stakes are so high, I believe it is necessary to seek a revelation regarding our triune God even though our Lord is one. This search must be motivated by the love we profess to have for Him. The Lord rewards those who diligently seek Him. It could be that the reward is the empowerment to live by faith because the Word He releases to you will be your light and your life.

If we are to seek His kingdom, first, let us all seek the King of kings and Lord of lords with all our hearts, minds, and souls. I pray that the pages that follow will ignite your faith and give you a thirst for more of Him. Even as you do so, you will find that other things in your life will align for your purpose in Him to be fulfilled. If you find His purpose, you shall find His provision.

Chapter 17

Love of God

For God so loved the world that He gave His only begotten Son, that whoever believes in Him should not perish but have everlasting life. John 3:16

Greater love has no one than this, than to lay down one's life for his friends. John 15:13

If you then, being evil, know how to give good gifts to your children, how much more will your heavenly Father give the Holy Spirit to those who ask Him! Luke 11:13

Jesus answered him, "The first of all the commandments is: 'Hear, O Israel, the Lord our God, the Lord is one. And you shall love the Lord your God with all your heart, with all your soul, with all your mind, and with all your strength.' This is the first commandment. And the second, like it, is this: 'You shall love your neighbor as yourself.' There is no other commandment greater than these." Mark 12:29–31

Whoever does not love does not know God, for God is love. 1 John 4:8

We love Him because He first loved us. If someone says, "I love God," and hates his brother, he is a liar; for he who does not love his brother whom he has seen, how can he love God whom he has not seen? And this commandment we have from Him: that he who loves God must love his brother also. 1 John 4:19–21

But I say to you, love your enemies, bless those who curse you, do good to those who hate you, and pray for those who spitefully use you and persecute you, that you may be sons of your Father in heaven. Matthew 5:44–45

One of the most important themes in and foundations of the Bible is the love of God. This love is quite different from the love that humans experience outside of God. First, it is experiential in the sense that you need to experience God to receive from God His love. Since it is so much of His nature, a continuous intimate relationship with Him will produce that impartation that will lead you to behave in a vastly different way.

A. You will become very forgiving toward your enemies. It is impossible to reach out to them in love and bless them through prayer or gifts if you have not already forgiven them. You will also become more forgiving toward your brothers and sisters in the Lord who do not agree with you and your theology.

B. You will become very generous toward people inside and outside the church. The love of God is clear in that He gives sacrificially of His best. He gave His Son, and then He gave His Holy Spirit. Don't ask God for the second best when He has His best for you. Any revelation of His love through sacrifice will lead you to love others through your sacrifice.

C. A revelation of His love through sacrifice will lead you to present yourself daily before God to surrender your life into His hands. There is a divine purpose for each one of your days on earth. I would write the previous sentence a thousand times. This is not about being prideful. It is about recognizing that God cares for you much more than you think. He cares about the plans He has for you. If your ministry is hidden, don't worry. Ministry is not about being popular with men and women but with God. The Lord rejoices in revealing Himself to you daily and revealing the great plans that He has for you.

In one of the many high points of revelation in Paul's life, he told us that it did not matter how many spiritual gifts and how much wisdom he might impart to others; without the love of God, he had nothing. In that chapter, he described the love of God (1 Corinthians 13) in quite different terms. The first words he used were *long-suffering* and *kind*. If you pay attention, many words are connected to our attitude toward others with the humility of God. It is impossible to remain prideful when constantly experiencing the love of God. In fact, you are burdened by lost souls and the need to build the church through faith. You connect with the plans of God as you connect with His love. Out of a love relationship, you discover your purpose.

Paul's prayer in Ephesians 3:19 was that we know experientially the love of God. He gave a three-dimensional picture that reminds us of the cross of Christ. The revelation of the cross is the revelation of the love of God. Paul said that he was crucified with Christ (Galatians 2:20). This surrender and sacrifice were encounters so transformational that with the love of God he could declare with confidence that it was the life of Christ he shared with others. Unless we are *only* motivated by the love of God, we will be motivated by other reasons.

Prayer:

Lord, I desire to know Your love like never before. Pour out Your love into me as you promised in the scriptures. Today, I surrender all self-seeking motivations, the desire for validation and honor that comes from men. I pray that You will refine my heart and reveal Your ways to me that I may not depart from them. I pray for a transformational revelation of Your humility on the cross. Give me grace to obey You in every circumstance.

Further Reading

To know the love of Christ which passes knowledge; that you may be filled with all the fullness of God. Ephesians 3:19

Now hope does not disappoint, because the love of God has been poured out in our hearts by the Holy Spirit who was given to us. Romans 5:5

But God demonstrates His own love toward us, in that while we were still sinners, Christ died for us. Romans 5:8

Chapter 18

Revelation of Christ as the Son of God

Simon Peter answered and said, "You are the Christ, the Son of the living God." Jesus answered and said to him, "Blessed are you, Simon Bar-Jonah, for flesh and blood has not revealed this to you, but My Father who is in heaven. And I also say to you that you are Peter, and on this rock I will build My church, and the gates of Hades shall not prevail against it." Matthew 16:16–18

When He had been baptized, Jesus came up immediately from the water; and behold, the heavens were opened to Him, and He saw the Spirit of God descending like a dove and alighting upon Him. And suddenly a voice came from heaven, saying, "This is My beloved Son, in whom I am well pleased." Matthew 3:16–17

This is My beloved Son, in whom I am well pleased. Hear Him! Matthew 17:5

The Lord your God will raise up for you a Prophet like me from your midst, from your brethren. Him you shall hear. Deuteronomy 18:15

So when the centurion and those with him, who were guarding Jesus, saw the earthquake and the things that had happened, they feared greatly, saying, "Truly this was the Son of God!" Matthew 27:54

Simon Bar-Jonah received a revelation from the Holy Spirit about Jesus. He had left everything to follow Jesus, so he was learning through obedience and by making mistakes. It was Peter's recognition of those mistakes that brought him closer to Jesus. However, it was not repentance for his lack of faith or seeing the miracles Jesus worked. It had to be the work of the Holy Spirit to provide the revelation of Jesus as the Son of God. Many people had suggestions about and interpretations of who Jesus could be, but Simon got it so right that the revelation changed his name. The meaning of Peter is *small rock*, and one metaphorical description of Jesus is *the cornerstone of the church*. In other words, Peter had become a part of the church by knowing the true identity of Jesus Christ.

Jesus made a declaration about His work. He builds the church through revelatory communication by the Holy Spirit and who He is as the Son of God. The more the church knows that truth, the more it is established. He also made a statement regarding victory over the gates of Hades. This is the final consequence of the revelation—victory over darkness by the power of God.

There are two key issues regarding Jesus Christ that will help us understand the work He is doing and see His provision in our lives. First, the declaration of the Father comes at a time when Jesus was baptized before men. This act of humility, receiving the promised Holy Spirit, opens the heavens. The Father declared Jesus to be His Son. If we want to really know Jesus, we need to understand what it means to humble ourselves and be filled with His Holy Spirit. Then we need to learn what it means to hear and obey what the Holy Spirit is telling us.

This issue of Jesus's identity as the Son of God was Satan's main point of temptation. In fact, the challenge was to reveal the power of God that Jesus's identity carries. Many times, people came to recognize Him as the Son of God because of the miracles He did. His position as Son is for the kingdom, and that kingdom is full of power.

Even though Jesus was tempted and recognized for His identity as the Son of God because of the miracles He worked, there were two key moments in His life where recognition came from both heaven and earth. Those moments were at His baptism and when He was on the cross. These were moments of complete obedience when Jesus showed us His humility. The lesson we can learn here is that when you obey God, and it leads to great humiliation, be confident that your Father will reveal your glory. It is at that moment that you will have intimate communion with Christ as the Son of God.

Prayer:
Lord, I pray that You reveal Yourself to me as the Son of God. I believe that You will continue Your work in me to finish the faith that You have started. May You live through me to demonstrate Your kingdom in power that many will be saved, healed, and delivered for Your glory.

Further Reading

> Now when the tempter came to Him, he said, "If You are the Son of God, command that these stones become bread." Matthew 4:3

> You who destroy the temple and build it in three days, save Yourself! If You are the Son of God, come down from the cross. Matthew 27:40

> Then those who were in the boat came and worshiped Him, saying, "Truly You are the Son of God." Matthew 14:33

Now it came to pass, as He sat at the table with them, that He took bread, blessed and broke it, and gave it to them. Then their eyes were opened and they knew Him; and He vanished from their sight. Luke 24:30–31

Chapter 19

Revelation of the Father

Philip said to Him, "Lord, show us the Father, and it is sufficient for us." Jesus said to him, "Have I been with you so long, and yet you have not known Me, Philip? He who has seen Me has seen the Father." John 14:8–9

All things have been delivered to Me by My Father, and no one knows the Son except the Father. Nor does anyone know the Father except the Son, and the one to whom the Son wills to reveal Him. Matthew 11:27

In this manner, therefore, pray: Our Father in heaven, hallowed be Your name. Matthew 6:9

"Come out from among them and be separate," says the Lord. "Do not touch what is unclean, and I will receive you. I will be a Father to you, and you shall be My sons and daughters," says the Lord Almighty. 2 Corinthians 6:17–18

But love your enemies, do good, and lend, hoping for nothing in return; and your reward will be

great, and you will be sons of the Most High. For
He is kind to the unthankful and evil. Therefore
be merciful, just as your Father also is merciful.
Luke 6:35–36

Even though the Father revealed Himself through Jesus, it was
Jesus's intention to lead us to the Father through Him. Jesus knows
that the Father sends a helper to guide us to the truth: the Holy Spirit.
Jesus's teaching on prayer is addressed to the Father. He affirms that
if we ask in His name, we can be sure that we will receive from the
Father.

It is Jesus's intention to reveal to us a Father who loves us, provides for us, and is interested in our future. He has plans for us that He
wants to reveal, but it is necessary that in order to come to that revelation of who we are as sons and daughters, we must come out of the
world to seek Him. In that relationship, the Father corrects and disci-
plines His children; but even in those moments, you will realize that it
is for your good and that you are being shaped in the image of His Son.

We learn from Jesus that the Father cares for our needs and that
we will be provided for as we seek His kingdom. To seek His kingdom is to seek Him as the Father, a rewarder of those who diligently
seek Him (Hebrews 11:6).

Biblical promises are there not only to be believed but also to be
acted upon. If you get close to God, He will also draw near to you. If
you humble yourself before God, He will lift you. If you pray to God
in secret, He will reward you. If you seek to honor the Father in your
giving, He will protect your finances and supply you with purpose
and provision. All of these promises are for believers so that God can
manifest His power through you.

Prayer:
*Father, I pray that You reveal Yourself to me in Christ. Give me the grace
to leave the world behind and fill me with Your spirit and the grace to
show love and mercy toward my enemies. I pray that Your will be done,
and Your kingdom come through me to set the captives free. Anoint me*

afresh and send me to the harvest to preach in Your name. I pray You will confirm Your Word with Your power in Jesus's name.

Further Reading

But if I do, though you do not believe Me, believe the works, that you may know and believe that the Father is in Me, and I in Him. John 10:38

Behold what manner of love the Father has bestowed on us, that we should be called children of God! 1 John 3:1

And in that day you will ask Me nothing. Most assuredly, I say to you, whatever you ask the Father in My name He will give you. John 16:23

Men of Israel, hear these words: Jesus of Nazareth, a Man attested by God to you by miracles, wonders, and signs which God did through Him in your midst, as you yourselves also know Acts 2:22

Therefore do not worry, saying, "What shall we eat?" or "What shall we drink?" or "What shall we wear?" For after all these things the Gentiles seek. For your heavenly Father knows that you need all these things. But seek first the kingdom of God and His righteousness, and all these things shall be added to you. Matthew 6:31–33

And you have forgotten the exhortation which speaks to you as to sons: "My son, do not despise the chastening of the Lord, nor be discouraged when you are rebuked by Him; for whom the Lord loves He chastens, and scourges every son whom He receives." Hebrews 12:5–6

Chapter 20

Revelation of the Holy Spirit

And I will pray the Father, and He will give you another Helper, that He may abide with you forever—the Spirit of truth, whom the world cannot receive, because it neither sees Him nor knows Him; but you know Him, for He dwells with you and will be in you. John 14:16–17

If you then, being evil, know how to give good gifts to your children, how much more will your heavenly Father give the Holy Spirit to those who ask Him! Luke 11:13

I still have many things to say to you, but you cannot bear them now. However, when He, the Spirit of truth, has come, He will guide you into all truth; for He will not speak on His own authority, but whatever He hears He will speak; and He will tell you things to come. John 16:12–13

Do not quench the Spirit. Do not despise prophecies. Test all things; hold fast what is good. Abstain from every form of evil. 1 Thessalonians 5:19–22

The Spirit of the Lord is upon Me, because He has anointed Me to preach the gospel to the poor; He has sent Me to heal the brokenhearted, to proclaim liberty to the captives and recovery of sight to the blind, to set at liberty those who are oppressed. Luke 4:18

The most important promise of Jesus Christ to His people is the promise of the Holy Spirit. Jesus did not intend for His people to walk in the truth without the Spirit. Not only does Jesus pray to the Father, He knows that the Father will send the Holy Spirit to us. Besides that, it is the will of the Father to give the Holy Spirit to those who ask of Him. There are many things that the Holy Spirit does through us. It speaks what Jesus declares, It speaks of the things to come, and It causes us to prophesy. In Thessalonians, we read that we should not quench the Spirit nor despise prophecies. Could it be because the Lord wants us to prophesy and believe in what the Holy Spirit is declaring to us? That is the promise He gave to us. He will tell us of things to come.

The reason the church is called the body of Christ is not only because Christ lives in us but also because we live in Him. Therefore, what He did when walking with His disciples, He also wants to continue doing through the church: preaching the gospel, healing the sick, and casting out demons. This is a manifestation of the power of God by the Holy Spirit to confirm the word He leads us to share.

You may be thinking that there is nothing new here. We know all this, but do we really know it? Is the church, in this day and time, a place of the manifestation of the Holy Spirit everywhere? Or could it be that we like to know about God and do something else instead of *knowing* God and doing His will? His kingdom comes, and His will is done because His is the power and the glory. The manifestation of His power will bring Him glory. That is His kingdom on earth.

To intimately know the Holy Spirit is to treasure His Word. Our investments of time, finances, and talent are all directed toward it. We delight in His Word and do what pleases Him. It is also to hate evil. We are new creations that hate sin. However, the flesh loves sin. It surrenders to the work of the Holy Spirit in us, for the circumcision of the heart is not done by a blade but by the fire of the Holy Spirit. Only those who have allowed the Holy Spirit to do the deep work of death in their hearts can receive resurrection in life. In Paul's life, we see how the Holy Spirit blinded him. We could think that He was punishing him by making him unable to lead the life he had led until then. However, it was by the grace of God that he was blinded so that his spiritual eyes could be open to seek God and receive from Him. In those three days of fasting and repentance, Paul sought to understand what the Lord would have him do. Great brokenness brings great revival in our lives.

I encourage you to submit to the Holy Spirit. He will lead you to truth in your heart so that when you speak, you will speak the truth. Be open to receive ideas for business breakthroughs. Know that every challenge that you are facing is first a challenge of faith. The challenge is saying, "Is the Lord going to help me now?" The Lord is near you, leading you into your miracle by His Spirit. Recognize His voice and obey Him. This is the secret of true prosperity.

Prayer:
Lord, I repent of my neglecting and despising the presence of the Holy Spirit in my life. I surrender to You, and I pray that the Holy Spirit will lead me to Your truth. Anoint me afresh today to speak your Word and give me the courage to believe in the miracles of healing and deliverance that will follow me. I pray for the wisdom to carry out my business for Your glory. I surrender my life and my business to You today.

Further Reading

> Let no corrupt word proceed out of your mouth, but what is good for necessary edification, that it may impart grace to the hearers. And do not grieve the Holy Spirit of God, by whom you were sealed for the day of redemption. Ephesians 4:29–30

Then Peter said to her, "How is it that you have agreed together to test the Spirit of the Lord? Look, the feet of those who have buried your husband are at the door, and they will carry you out." Acts 5:9

Therefore I say to you, every sin and blasphemy will be forgiven men, but the blasphemy against the Spirit will not be forgiven men. Anyone who speaks a word against the Son of Man, it will be forgiven him; but whoever speaks against the Holy Spirit, it will not be forgiven him, either in this age or in the age to come. Matthew 12:31–32

There shall come forth a Rod from the stem of Jesse, and a Branch shall grow out of his roots. The Spirit of the Lord shall rest upon Him, the Spirit of wisdom and understanding, the Spirit of counsel and might, the Spirit of knowledge and of the fear of the Lord. Isaiah 11:1–2

Chapter 21

Revelation of the Church

For he who eats and drinks in an unworthy manner eats and drinks judgment to himself, not discerning the Lord's body. 1 Corinthians 11:29

But whoever causes one of these little ones who believe in Me to stumble, it would be better for him if a millstone were hung around his neck, and he were thrown into the sea. Mark 9:42

Bear one another's burdens, and so fulfill the law of Christ. Galatians 6:2,

The revelation of the body of Christ will lead us to behave according to the Word. Right now, do we really see one another as "members of one another?" What are the practical steps we take daily to help the needy and honor one another and our leaders?

1 Corinthians 11 shows that how we treat one another matters to God. In fact, the Bible is filled with practical information about how to support, help, encourage, and bless each one another in many ways. The story of the good Samaritan in Luke 10 is a good example of how an unexpected person is able to break a cultural boundary (Jews versus Samaritans) and reach out to help a dying man who had been robbed and hurt.

The good Samaritan does God's work in many ways. He (a) invests much time; (b) uses his own healing products; (c) performs healing services; and (d) provides transport and food and lodging for the future, not caring how much it might cost him. This is extravagant generosity that brings complete restoration. The good Samaritan's purpose was to find a way to help one person. How are we expressing that God has commanded us to love one another?

One of the key questions that we need to ask ourselves as we continue to live out the revelation of the church to the world concerns our motivation. What is the deep motivation that moves us to work and interact with one another? If it is not the love of God, we may be unaware of a hidden agenda that has been planted in us by the world's value system. Ephesians 4 conveys the idea of ministers, equipping the saints for spiritual work, where *everyone* has a role to play in the edification of a spiritual body in love. If love is not the purpose and result of the function of that body, there are other purposes and results. If the church is a pillar of truth, that truth needs to be revealed to its members so that they might walk in the truth.

I suggest that, in the days to come, we are going to need to experience a revelation of apostolic and prophetic gifts and anointing, aligning ourselves with the Lord in love, humility, and truth. True spiritual relationships that build people up in the way they experience the power and purpose of God will become essential in that hour. It is the end of empty flattering and time for true honor, which opens the way to receiving and treasuring the Word that the Lord has for us.

Prayer:
Lord, help me discern the body of Christ and become an instrument of influence, bringing Your love and truth to the world. I pray that You help me encourage my brothers and sisters in need and enable me to be a blessing to them in every way I can. May You be glorified as all provision comes from You. I pray that You help me find my place and role in the church so that I can fulfill the purpose You have for me. I pray for the harvest of souls and blessings You have for them.

Further Reading

From whom the whole body, joined and knit together by what every joint supplies, according to the effective working by which every part does its share, causes growth of the body for the edifying of itself in love. Ephesians 4:16

I write so that you may know how you ought to conduct yourself in the house of God, which is the church of the living God, the pillar and ground of the truth. 1 Timothy 3:15

Honor widows who are really widows. 1 Timothy 5:3

Now, therefore, you are no longer strangers and foreigners, but fellow citizens with the saints and members of the household of God, having been built on the foundation of the apostles and prophets, Jesus Christ Himself being the chief cornerstone, in whom the whole building, being fitted together, grows into a holy temple in the Lord, in whom you also are being built together for a dwelling place of God in the Spirit. Ephesians 2:19–22

Be kindly affectionate to one another with brotherly love, in honor giving preference to one another. Romans 12:10

Let the elders who rule well be counted worthy of double honor, especially those who labor in the word and doctrine. 1 Timothy 5:17

But whoever has this world's goods, and sees his brother in need, and shuts up his heart from him, how does the love of God abide in him? 1 John 3:17

Therefore, putting away lying, "Let each one of you speak truth with his neighbor," for we are members of one another. Ephesians 4:25

Chapter 22

Eternal Rewards

So Jesus said to them, "Assuredly I say to you, that in the regeneration, when the Son of Man sits on the throne of His glory, you who have followed Me will also sit on twelve thrones, judging the twelve tribes of Israel. And everyone who has left houses or brothers or sisters or father or mother or wife or children or lands, for My name's sake, shall receive a hundredfold, and inherit eternal life." Matthew 19:28–29

He who overcomes shall inherit all things, and I will be his God and he shall be My son. Revelation 21:7

Many of the promises that Jesus gave to His disciples and to us are not for today. They are for a time to come. We need to pay careful attention to this, lest all our prayers and expectations be targeted toward receiving a reward for our life on earth, and we miss the better rewards that are for eternity.

In both Matthew 19:28 and Revelation 2:26, Jesus tells us that we can join Him in His work in the regeneration, doing what He has called us to do: judge cities and have influence over nations. This seems a high calling that would require us to use this life as preparation, investing ourselves wholly in His kingdom. There are far greater rewards that we cannot understand now because we do not possess a heavenly perspective. However, we need to continue to pray and seek God because, in full obedience, we will fulfill God's call for our generation.

Many other scriptures mention eternal rewards, and some of them are listed below. Abraham looked for a city whose architect and builder was God (Hebrews 11:10), he but did not get to see it because he looked for eternal rewards. Many other saints did not receive the promises (Hebrews 11:39), for we enter into those promises with them. It seems that we have been blinded to them, for we are too much focused on our current reality. I suggest we continue to seek the scriptures and visualize, believe in, and work toward those rewards, for those promises are also valuable.

Prayer:
Lord, I pray that You give me a revelation of eternal rewards. I pray that You remove unnecessary attachments to this world and that You lead me along a path of consecration to serve You fully as I know it is my duty and privilege to do so. I pray that You will open doors for me so that I might bring the gospel to the unreached, to the neediest, and to other nations. Help me be aware of the leadership of the Spirit and connect with people of the same mind. Reveal Your love to me and transform me so that people will see Christ working through me to bless people.

Further Reading

> And he who overcomes, and keeps My works until the end, to him I will give power over the nations—"He shall rule them with a rod of iron; They shall be dashed to pieces like the potter's vessels"—as I also have received from My Father. Revelation 2:26–27

> For we must all appear before the judgment seat of Christ, that each one may receive the things

done in the body, according to what he has done, whether good or bad. 2 Corinthians 5:10

And behold, I am coming quickly, and My reward is with Me, to give to every one according to his work. Revelation 22:12

And when the Chief Shepherd appears, you will receive the crown of glory that does not fade away. 1 Peter 5:4

Chapter 23

Conclusion

He made known His ways to Moses, His acts to the children of Israel. Psalm 103:7

Wisdom is the principal thing; Therefore, get wisdom. And in all your getting, get understanding. Proverbs 4:7

He who did not spare His own Son, but delivered Him up for us all, how shall He not with Him also freely give us all things? Romans 8:32

And all these blessings shall come upon you and overtake you, because you obey the voice of the Lord your God. Deuteronomy 28:2

I have been sharing on the topic of tithes and offerings for many years, and I've noticed that I continue to reinforce two key interrelated messages. It is not about what we give to the Lord; it is how we give it to Him. It is not about money; it is about faith. We need to become aware of the value system that drives us in every act of giving, be it of our finances, time, or talent.

I will use the analogy of a box with a gift inside. If it isn't aligned to our actions and pure motives, much of what we gather about God in our minds and in what we say is just the box. A beautiful box may lead you to think that there is a beautiful gift inside, but that may not be so. An ugly box may lead you to think that there is a mediocre gift inside. Our true value system guides our daily actions. Are we really motivated by the love of God and led by the Spirit in what we do?

We have to ask God for the discernment to understand our hearts, for the knowledge to clearly perceive and receive His word, and for wisdom to apply it through His Spirit. This is Paul's prayer in Ephesians 1. May that be our daily prayer because we cannot do it without Him.

Through the lives of normal people such as Moses and Joshua, the Lord reminds us of the importance of hearing and following His Word and the rewards that He has for everyone who obeys Him. The Lord has true wealth for those who follow Him because He manifests His true wealth in you and to the people around you through you.

It is in seeking God and obeying what He tells you to do that you will find the type of prosperity He has secured for you. I encourage you to seek the Lord to reveal more of Him to you. Your heart will be transformed into a heart devoted to Him, feeling His burden for His people, your community, your nation, and other nations. You will learn to appreciate heavenly treasures and everything that He has freely given to you, but you have not yet learned to appreciate.

Truly knowing God will allow you to effortlessly make Him truly known. There will be such a grace poured over your life that you will not know what has happened to you. Praying, fasting, worshipping, evangelizing, and caring for people will all be easy once your heart is truly converted to Him. There will be a moment of revelation of the Father where you will begin to receive so many blessings that you will feel dizzy and perplexed, for such is the love the Lord has for you. Take your position as His child, believe, and declare His greatness and goodness. A truly intimate relationship with Him will lead you into brokenness, repentance, and fruitfulness.

My prayer for you:
I pray that the Lord will use this book to bless you beyond your wildest dreams that you will become a true spokesperson for the gospel of Jesus Christ because you live His life. I also pray that you will find a hunger

and thirst for righteousness that leads you to sow bountifully with good works in His name. I pray an end to dissension and strife over finances at home and in the church, that the peace of the Lord will fill you, and that you will move in His power and wisdom. He will empower you to speak to the mountain, and the mountain will move. I pray that the Lord will give you divine perspective over every situation and every relationship that His light and wisdom will shine through you to turn hearts to Him. Finally, I pray that you will find wealth in Christ who is in you, a hope of glory to empower you to do all things.

Further Reading

If any of you lacks wisdom, let him ask of God, who gives to all liberally and without reproach, and it will be given to him. James 1:5

The fear of the Lord is the beginning of knowledge, but fools despise wisdom and instruction. Proverbs 1:7

Receive my instruction, and not silver, and knowledge rather than choice gold; for wisdom is better than rubies, and all the things one may desire cannot be compared with her. Proverbs 8:10–11

Chapter 24

Next Steps

Have I not commanded you? Be strong and of
good courage; do not be afraid, nor be dismayed,
for the Lord your God is with you wherever you
go. Joshua 1:9

I advise you to read the book of Joshua because we are about to
enter our promised land, and there is much work to do for everyone
who is willing.

There are a few things you can do to start changing your habits.
In this section, I suggest a few. If you disagree, I accept that, but then I
ask that you give me a different set of steps. Doing nothing is not a step.

1. Start small. Think of small changes you can make con-
   sistently. If you are not used to giving, start giving small
   amounts to different causes in the church. For instance, a
   five-dollar tithe, a five-dollar pastoral offering (giving leaders double honor), five-dollar benevolence (taking care of
   the poor), or a five-dollar mission (helping to bring the
   message of the gospel to nations). Those are small offerings
   full of purpose and faith.
2. Pray over the offering you give before you give it. Your prayer
   should be that the Lord will use it for the extension of His

kingdom. In other words, every week, your offering should be a reason to engage your faith in seeking God's kingdom.

3. Give to brothers and sisters in need. If you don't have much, then give a small offering. Your sacrifice will move God's hand.

4. Pray for your brothers and sisters in need. Make it clear that you are not the solution to their problems, but rather God is. As you pray over the offering with the love of and faith in God, the Lord will see that as an open door to bless your brothers and sisters. Don't give money, give faith. When God answers the prayer, all the praise will go to Him and not to you, and that is a good thing.

5. Surrender your business to the Lord and ask Him for guidance. Your employees watch your life. Your actions are (or are not) a gospel message to them. The Lord will guide you to do unusual things for them (such as give them a blessed treatment that nobody else does), and He will step into their lives so that they will become more productive and committed to the company.

6. Sow in faith every day, and it will become a habit.

7. Give this book to someone who will benefit from reading it, and tell them to do the same when they are done. This book is not intended to gather dust on a shelf.

8. Connect with people who have the gift of giving and ask them to pray for you. Get to know them and ask them why and how they give.

9. If you have sown in faith, remind God of those seeds. A prayer about your faithful giving is not a sign of pride, but a sign of faith.

10. Don't give beyond your faith. Don't put offerings on a credit card that you cannot pay. Giving is from the heart. If you love God, He will put in your heart how to sow more and in different ways. You will become a bountiful giver, and you won't feel any remorse about it. You will not give out of compulsion but from conviction.

My prayer is that these steps will trigger more ideas in you and that you will find your own God-given strategy to become an amazing blessing to the kingdom of God. Since it is more blessed to give than to receive, I wanted to share much on that topic. However, I do have three insights to share with you about receiving:

1. Refuse to think small. Think big, and once that thought is concrete in your mind, think bigger.
2. Don't despise small gifts that come to you because you cannot know the sacrifice and faith that is behind them.
3. Don't be too proud to refuse any gift by saying, "The Lord is my provider." It is the Lord who is sending you someone to provide for you.

In the next few pages, I suggest a few resources that will help your church grow.

If you want to read more about and get involved with our latest work, you can find us at the following:

1. Kingdom Finances Facebook group: https://www.facebook.com/Kingdom-Finances2264-111286683927430/
2. Kingdom Finances Website: kingdomfinances.us
3. Kingdom Finances Testimonials: A Project to Transform Communities

   a. Purpose: compilation of testimonies to bless the church
   b. Contact Hector Ramos at hreina@gmail.com for more information.

4. Kingdom Finances: Training, Facilitation, Coaching, Mentoring

Benefits:
   a. Clarify the vision
   b. Develop a strategy

     c. Discern divine help
     d. Build faith in God's plan and provision
     e. Learn how to coach others
     f. Increase productivity
     g. Increase accountability
     h. Receive impartation
     i. Experience testimony

Structure:
     a. Presentation
     b. Group work
     c. Small group coaching

Strategy:
     a. Prayer
     b. Revelation
     c. Implementation
     d. Testimony

System:
     a. Jesus's approach to coaching and mentoring
     b. Growth model of coaching
     c. Basic principles of mentoring
     d. Group work and work in pairs

Length: three months / six months / twelve months
Maximum number of participants per cohort: twenty-four

5. Creative Thinking and Church Growth Workshop

Purpose: Leverage the creative potential of the congregation to generate possible solutions to community challenges. This is done prayerfully, hearing from God and submitting plans to God.
Maximum number of participants: 250
Length: one to two days

6. Kingdom Finances: New Business Development

Purpose: Help identify talents, strengths, and potential skills in individuals and teams to build businesses.

Structure:
>Kingdom values
>Business models
>Minimum value offering
>Unique value proposition
>Competitive advantage
>Social corporate responsibility
>Faith applied to business
>The bigger picture

This program includes presentations from experts from different industries to help explain key information that will assist with developing business solutions.
Length: six months
Maximum number of participants: twelve

About the Author

Originally from Madrid, Spain, Hector has ministered prophetically in Singapore, Malaysia, Indonesia, India, United Arab Emirates, Estonia, Russia, and the United States. His passion is to empower the body of Christ with faith for resources to build the Church and to minister in missional work including the marketplace. He is currently serving as associate pastor at the Equipping Church, Bryan, Texas. He writes on the subject of kingdom finances on his blog KingdomFinances.us.

Hector holds a PhD in educational psychology from Texas A&M University, focusing on creativity, intelligence, and giftedness. He previously earned his MS degree in creative studies and change leadership from the State University of New York, Buffalo. His research deals with the effects of cognitive fixation on pastoral leadership. He facilitates creative thinking workshops for the church in crafting a personal and corporate vision and designing innovative solutions for challenges faced by the church.

Hector is a lecturer of innovative and creative thinking, educational psychology, and survey research at Texas A&M University. He has worked with Buffalo State College to instruct school teachers in Kuwait and Mexico as part of a master's in educational leadership. In addition, Hector works as a creative thinking coach with business clients from different nations.

Printed in the USA
CPSIA information can be obtained
at www.ICGtesting.com
LVHW041103150724
785543LV00019B/128